Don't Be A Victim!

An Officer's Advice on Preventing Crime

by

John Elliott

PrepperPress

Your Survival Library

www.PrepperPress.com

Don't Be A Victim!

An Officer's Advice on Preventing Crime

ISBN 978-0615766034

Copyright © 2013 by John Elliott

All rights reserved.

Printed in the United States of America.

Prepper Press Trade Paperback Edition: February 2013

Prepper Press is a division of Northern House Media, LLC

- *To my two daughters, Mia and Illianna; my grandchildren, Francesca, Autumn, Paris, Glennon and Collin; and the love of my life, Marlene.*

About the Author

A law enforcement veteran, John Elliott worked for police agencies in Virginia, Rhode Island and Florida, as well as for the U.S. Department of Justice and the U.S. Customs Service. He also spent many years working with Interpol, and was a bomb disposal technician conducting land mine and unexploded military ordnance disposal in the Middle East, Eastern Europe, Asia and North Africa. Fourty-four of those years was spent working in concert with the U.S. State Department's Office of Special Investigations and with Mossad in Israel.

He holds a Bachelor of Science in Business, an MBA and a Juris Doctorate degree. He is the proud father of two daughters and five grandchildren.

Foreword

During my twenty-four years as a Police Officer, I learned that when you show a criminal vulnerability, he/she will not hesitate to take advantage of you and turn you into a victim of crime.

Have you ever had anything stolen from you? Ever been face-to-face with a thief? It is a feeling that you will never ever forget, a feeling of being violated, knowing that someone had the audacity to break into your home and steal something that you worked so hard to earn. Then, in a matter of minutes, it is gone. Emotions of all kinds overwhelm you at once. You're angry, upset and you want to find the person who committed this act – *right now* – so that justice can be served. We never take the time to assess the fact that maybe this crime could have been prevented if we had been more alert, if we'd taken steps to protect the home or automobile a little better.

You then begin to ask yourself, why was I the criminal's target? What did I do to deserve this? The answer is nothing. Crime does not care about your race, social standing, economic status, or your religious belief. If you are not careful, crime may come to your door, and if it does, it will not knock before entering. Once you realize that crime does not discriminate, you will be able to empower yourself, protect your family and your property.

In his latest book, *Don't be a Victim*, John Elliott takes you step-by-step through various methods to reduce the chances you will be a victim of crime. He dives into the criminal mind, how it functions, what it thinks. John Elliott explains in a very simple way with many examples how to protect yourself and use good common sense so that you will not end up a victim.

This book can serve as a handbook for you and your family on how to be safe and alert. I encourage every reader to pass this book along to their family, neighbors and friends.

While the book in and of itself is not a silver bullet, John Elliott has done an exceptional job capturing the basic principles on how to protect yourself. This book will empower you. *Don't Be a Victim* is a book that should be included in everyone's personal library.

-     Ken Jefferson Retired Police Officer, Expert Crime Analyst WJXT TV 4

Jacksonville, FL 32013

Table of Contents

Chapter One

The Reality

When was the last time you or your family felt secure enough to leave your house unlocked in order to take a leisurely stroll through your neighborhood? When was the last time you took a walk anywhere at night? If you're a baby boomer like me, the answer to either of those questions is "maybe twenty or thirty years ago."

The overriding feeling of uneasiness many people have at being outside during the hours of darkness, whether taking a stroll around the neighborhood or walking to the car in the mall parking lot at 10:00 p.m., is undeniable, and has become widespread. Like it or not, we have become a society of victims. The fears that we feel are real. It is not a matter of an overactive imagination that fuels the fears; it's a matter of reality.

In my family, for instance, five people have been victimized in one fashion or another. Most of the people I know have relatives or friends who have also been victimized. And I'm fairly sure that since you are reading this book, you, too, have either been a victim, know someone who is a victim, or are concerned enough about these issues to take some simple steps to avoid becoming a victim. Hopefully the latter is true.

In the following pages, you will be given an inside look at the crimes, the criminals and the victims. You will also be shown the simple steps that can be taken to elevate yourself and your family above that victim category.

About Crime

No matter what politicians want us to believe, crime is absolutely not on the decrease. Ken Sikora, a retired police officer who knows what he's talking about, once told me, "As a former police officer, I can truly say things are not getting better on the streets, no matter what some statistics may say. Statistics can be read to say anything the writer wants them to say. It's all in the proper wording[1]."

---

[1] Sikora, Ken. Private conversations. Las Vegas. 2003, 2012.

Ken is 100 percent correct. Depending on who is in political office at the time and, of course, depending on whether or not it's an election year, you may hear that the crime rate is very low, is in decline or is only slightly on the increase. The reality is, however, that in most cases and in most geographical locations, crime has indeed increased at an alarming rate. Those increases include all the serious crime categories such as murder, rape and robbery, as well as burglaries, home invasions (with its associated violence) and carjackings. Assault and battery, drug use and prostitution are also on the rise[2].

According to Justice Department figures, in the United States there are well over 40 million personal and household crimes committed each year[3]. Violent crimes occur every 1.2 seconds, and violence directed toward women now occurs on the average of every 7 seconds.

It is important to understand that the victims of these crimes are not just the poor or displaced. They range in age all the way from infants to the elderly. They include the middle class and the wealthy. Many of the victims of home invasions are wealthy. Thefts occur on the average of one every 0.8 seconds, and burglaries every 4.9 seconds.

There are about 600,000 law enforcement officers in the United States, but because of scheduling for days off and vacations, only about 100,000 are actually on duty at any given time. Of that figure, the total number of police officers, deputy sheriffs, marshals and constables who are actually patrolling our streets and arresting criminals is about 65,000. The remaining 35,000 or so are involved in all of the ancillary work, including gathering and researching evidence, maintaining records, dispatching other officers, making court appearances and managing personnel. So, you can see that, for a country the size of the United States, there are only a small number of police officers actively involved in crime prevention.

During the former Clinton Administration, there was a promise of an additional 100,000 police officers to patrol the country's streets. That promised federal funding soon ran short; it would have eventually been up to the taxpayers to fund the increase. We never did get the extra police officers, but the President's promise sure sounded

---

[2] United States. Department of Justice. *Quarterly Review*. Washington, DC: Bureau of Justice Standards, November, 2011. Print.

[3] United States. Department of Justice. *Quarterly Review*. Washington, DC: Bureau of Justice Standards, 2011. Print.

good to a whole bunch of voters that year.

Crime is a global problem that affects all of us. In 1996, I was in Bosnia-Herzegovina training Croatian, Muslim and Serbian police officers. During a 72-hour leave in Zagreb, I was approached by an elderly Croatian lady whose handbag was taken from her while she was walking down a busy city street. The young thief ran away with her life savings. Over the next couple of days, I managed to obtain donations from many of the personnel stationed at the military installation of Camp Pleso. Her new life savings— twice the amount that was stolen— were placed in a similar handbag purchased at the base exchange. When the handbag was presented to her, she broke into tears. She related how she and many others were the frequent victims of crimes including muggings, rape and robbery, and said that the police were, for the most part, ineffective and uncaring. For my part, I found that the Croatian police were actually extremely professional and thorough, but they, like most law enforcement agencies throughout the world, are overwhelmed by the volume of crime.

A good friend of mine is a police officer in Italy. She often points to her country's rising crime rate and the almost desperate measures its police sometimes take in their continual fight against the criminal element. Many of the Italian police forces have become camouflage-clad commando units. Their elite Carabinieri have specialized groups that are trained to deal with a variety of problems including the Mafia, domestic terrorism, narcotics manufacturing and smuggling.

Another friend, a German police lieutenant, told me that his agency is so overburdened with major case investigations (murder, rape and robbery) that they have little time for the proper investigations of other crimes, such as burglary and theft. Many agencies, including many right here in the United States, are turning to the unproven method of taking misdemeanor crime reports right over the telephone.

A cousin of mine is a police officer in Scotland. He recently told me that he remembers the time when he could leave his house unlocked, drive down to the village, leave the car unlocked while shopping, leave his purchases in the unlocked car while having lunch in a café, and then return home to find everything as he left it. He said that if he did that today, he's sure he would find his car and everything in it stolen, and that, returning home, he'd find his house burglarized and vandalized. He added that since Scotland gained its independence in 2000, there have been some moves to arm the police. With the exception of some specialized units, the police in Scotland, Ireland and England are unarmed. But this is changing, and a recent heated discussion in Parliament regarding the rising tide of crime pointed to the very real possibility that the familiar London bobbies will soon be armed.

Should we hire more police officers? Should we in some fashion assist the police? The answer to both those questions is a resounding "Yes!" But to a great degree part of the solution rests on *our* shoulders. It is not enough to expect law enforcement officers to do the job alone. We must, at some point, take control of our lives and not allow ourselves to become victims. And we must use some degree of good common sense.

Police are often called to handle a variety of situations that are sometimes way beyond their job description. As a police officer, I have lost count of the times when anguished parents have called the police department demanding that an officer respond and make little Jimmy or Julie attend school.

While patrolling city streets, I often saw very young children left unattended, sometimes late at night. Where were the parents? Most of them were sitting at home, completely unaware of the child's situation. It begs the question, do these parents really care? If you were to ask them, they would be offended by the very suggestion that they didn't. But the awful reality is that many parents do not really care at all. If something were to happen to one of these children, however, it would be those same parents who would be screaming the loudest about how the police department had somehow failed in its responsibility to protect the child.

The police cannot, and should not, be the social workers for all the ills of the world. We must allow the police to police our country, and not run social feel better programs just because some local politicians believe it is the proper thing to do.

Who Are the Criminals?

My personal experience during my forty-four years of law enforcement work has taught me that the majority of criminals are people ranging in age from the late teens to the late fifties. Criminals are not necessarily brave people. They are the pariahs of the world, and as such will prey on whomever they can, whenever they think they can get away with it. A recent study published in the Department of

Justice's quarterly review for January 2011 concluded that for every twenty people in this country who are honest, hardworking and law abiding, there are one or two others who have some sort of criminal intent. In some areas the figure is closer to one in ten[4]. Police officers in Florida can tell you that for every five cars they stop for traffic infractions, one of them probably contains a fugitive from somewhere, an illegal alien, a driver with a suspended or revoked driver's license, someone with an arrest warrant, illegal drugs and/or a gun in the car, or the car itself is stolen[5].

Increasingly, the perpetrators are younger each year. It is not unusual these days to hear about a ten- or twelve-year-old boy arrested for murder or a child who brings a pistol into his elementary school to threaten his teacher or classmates. The Warwick, Rhode Island, police department reported in 1989 that a thirteen-year-old boy had burglarized a neighborhood home and stabbed to death the twenty-seven-year-old homeowner[6]. A mother of two small children, the victim was stabbed fifty-eight times with a knife taken from the kitchen. The child was not caught, and two years later, he stabbed to death three more neighbors (two of them were children). This time he was caught, and he eventually pled guilty to all four murders. However, he was sentenced as a juvenile and has since been paroled. Will he kill again? In my opinion, he will absolutely kill more people. Fortunately, the cases involving young children as the perpetrators are still relatively infrequent, according to the U.S. Department of Justice's Office of Juvenile Justice and Delinquency Prevention.

The criminal is not always easy to spot. Most criminals look pretty ordinary. Most of them blend in with everyone else. A veteran of the war in Vietnam once told me that the enemy was sometimes difficult or impossible to spot. "They looked just like everyone else," he said. Well, I can tell you quite frankly that the criminals are the enemy, and they do not all look like Charles Manson. If you were expecting all of them to be wearing a mask or to speak in a low gruff voice, then you would be mistaken. And they definitely do not appear as portrayed on television.

---

[4] United States. Department of Justice. *Quarterly Review*. Washington, DC: Bureau of Justice Standards, 2011. Print.

[5] State of Florida. *Statistical Analysis – 2009 to 2010*. Florida: Department of Law Enforcement. 2011. Print.

[6] Warwick Police Department, Rhode Island, 1989.

As an aside, I will tell you that for the purposes of this book, I usually refer to a criminal or criminals in the male gender. I use the words "he" and "his" quite a lot. But don't be misled — criminals come in both varieties, male and female. One of the most frightening people I had anything to do with was a woman arrested in a biker bar in Port Orange, Florida. She was a serial killer who had murdered a number of men who had unfortunately picked her up as she hitched rides throughout central Florida. Her eyes looked completely lifeless and blank, like the eyes of a shark. I'm certain that given the opportunity that evening, she would have been more than happy to take my life as well.

Criminals also range in age from the very young to the elderly. We can identify, generally speaking, what sort of person will commit what sort of crime. As an example, I used to conduct seminars for bank employees and was able to provide them with a general description of what the bank robber will look like. He is usually a white male between the ages of twenty-five to thirty-eight. He is usually of average height, and just slightly overweight. His usual disguise is a baseball cap and sunglasses. He will sometimes wear a fake moustache, but normally would not. He is usually dressed in blue jeans and a nondescript T-shirt that is not tucked in, but on rare occasions will be wearing a suit and tie (sans the baseball cap). He will be nervous and speak quickly to one teller in a voice barely audible to others. He will sometimes display a handgun, usually a semi-automatic, dark blue or black in color, but will sometimes only suggest that he is armed.

His car will be parked away from the bank. If the bank is in a strip-mall shopping center-type of arrangement shared by stores and restaurants, the car may be parked four or five rows away. And it will be parked so that he does not have to back out of a parking space, but can simply just drive forward. The most common time for bank robberies is mid- to late-morning and in the early afternoon.

The usual robber of a convenience store, on the other hand, is a black male in his mid- to late-teens or up to thirty years of age. He is usually wearing blue jeans with any assortment of shirt or jacket. He is usually armed with a revolver, dark blue or black, or chrome in color, and the weapon is normally displayed. The robber is usually extremely excited and animated, and may be shouting loudly. The robber usually lives in the general vicinity of the store and may leave the area on foot, as in the case of younger robbers. The most common time for convenience-store robberies is between 10:00 p.m. and 2:00 a.m.

There are, of course, exceptions to every rule. I once apprehended a bank robber who was sitting in his station wagon behind the bank, counting the money that he had just stolen. The man was sixty-two years old and was the manager of the ice cream store located right next to the bank.

Crime-Prevention Strategies

As a police officer in one capacity or another for thirty-seven years, I have come to understand that preventing victimization is not complicated and does not necessarily involve a great deal of technical equipment. It does, however, involve the implementation of a few simple safety tactics and some good common sense.

Often people may be oblivious to some very real dangers. I remember the case of a middle-aged professional woman who was driving on the interstate on her way home from work. A truck pulled up alongside her car, and the driver excitedly motioned for her to pull over as he pointed to the back of her car. The lady pulled over, but wisely stayed locked in her car with the windows rolled up. The driver of the truck stopped behind her and approached the side of her car. He yelled that her tire was going flat, and told her that he would change the tire. Instead of getting out of the car, the woman drove away and took the next exit to a garage. As it turned out, her tires were fine, and she most assuredly saved herself from a violent crime by following her instincts.

I have seen the victims of auto theft acting bewildered by what happened, never mind that they left the car unlocked or the windows rolled down, or even the keys in the ignition. "But I was just in the store for a minute!" is the common wail. As well, burglary victims are often mystified that their home was broken into, even though they left first-floor windows unlocked or open, or left the back door unsecured. So, the question comes to mind, what, generally speaking, can we do to enhance our safety and protect ourselves from the criminals?

The professional woman on the interstate had part of the answer. Her intuition paid off. She denied the criminal the access that he needed to reach her and the interior of her car. The one mistake she did make, and one that could have been fatal, was that she pulled over and stopped at all. It would have been much wiser to continue driving, and if she thought there may be a problem with her car, to drive immediately to a garage or other well-lit and crowded area. Instead, she pulled over and gave access, albeit limited, to the criminal. The criminal was smart enough to park his truck behind her, denying her the ability to see his license plate or to get a good look at the truck. The woman was extremely lucky. The man could have immediately shot her or broken the driver's side window to reach her.

We must understand that when crime happens, it happens very quickly. If you are the target of a robber, rapist, mugger or murderer, you will have little or no warning. According to most police reporting agencies, a purse snatcher takes about one to two seconds to complete his crime. A robbery can take as little as ten seconds, and that can include the time that you are knocked to the ground and beaten. Generally speaking, criminals are not the smartest people in the world. In the words of a retired New York City police officer, "They're not brain surgeons," but they are usually much better prepared than their victims.

The criminal already has a plan formulated in his mind. He knows who or what the target is, he knows what he wants to take or do, and he usually already knows his escape route. The victim, on the other hand, with no forewarning, is an easy target—just what the criminal is looking for.

As you read this book you will be given specific instructions about what to do to avoid being the victim of a variety of crimes, but there are four hard-and-fast rules to follow that will get you through almost anything the criminal has to offer:

1. Always be aware of your surroundings. Be alert.

2. Always know what to do ahead of time.

3. Do not allow criminals access to you, your family, your car or your home.

4. Believe in yourself and your instincts. Use common sense.

Be Aware

The most important thing to remember is to stay alert wherever you are. Not paranoid—just alert. Most unpleasant situations and encounters can be avoided by simply being aware of what's going on around you. This may take a little practice, but it can become second nature and it can keep you from becoming a victim.

> Look for avenues of escape.

> Practice seeing people as criminals.

> Be mindful of others who might approach you on foot, or who may drive slowly by you as you are walking down the street.

> Keep an eye out for pedestrian traffic behind you. When passing glass store fronts, take the opportunity to use the glass as a mirror.

> Learn to walk with your head held high, shoulders back, and with a steady purposeful stride.

> Be determined and resolute. Criminals will shy away from you. They will go to the man or woman who appears weak or preoccupied.

> When walking beside a roadway, whether in the city or the suburbs, walk against the traffic. This makes it more difficult for the criminal who may be in a car, motorcycle or bicycle and driving with the flow of traffic.

> If you are carrying a purse, make sure that the strap is over your head or shoulder, and carry the purse under your arm and against your body. If the purse has a flap for an opening, try to keep the flap side against your body. You could even carry the purse or handbag under your coat.

> Consider carrying your money, credit cards, driver's license and keys in a secure pocket and not in a purse. If a purse or handbag is taken from you, you have not lost a great deal, and the thief will not find out where you live.

> If you carry a wallet in your back pocket, make sure that the button on the pocket is secure. Consider putting your credit cards in a pocket and not in the wallet. Also consider leaving your cash (bills) folded in a pocket.

Be especially on alert in parking lots. If you're leaving the mall or the office late at night, and the parking lot is not well lit, either go with a group of people or have a security guard walk you to your car. Otherwise:

➢ Be ever mindful as you walk out into the lot of anyone who may be hiding behind a vehicle or in the shadows nearby.

➢ If there are no other people around and the security guard is not available, plan your approach to your car. Look for your car; try to determine if there are any other cars or people in the area.

➢ If there are people on foot near your car, and acting suspiciously, do not go into the parking lot. Call the police and ask them send a patrol car by. (They get paid for this, you know!)

➢ Do not walk out into the parking lot if there is a car parked next to yours, especially if the parking lot is almost empty, or if the car next to yours is parked so that it blocks the view of your car. When in doubt, call the police.

➢ If you *must* walk out into the lot alone, have your keys ready in your hand, not just the group of keys, but have the *actual* car key ready.

➢ If there is a car parked next to yours and you have to walk around it, give the vehicle a wide berth. Walk in an exaggerated arc around the suspicious car. Walk with a quick, confident and purposeful stride.

➢ Walk directly to your car, get in and lock the doors. Start the car moving right away. Do not take time to adjust the radio or anything else.

These measures may seem somewhat obvious and maybe a bit extreme, but if you're the victim of a robbery then all of a sudden they make perfect sense, as things you *should have* done.

Be Ready

It is very important that you have a plan formulated ahead of time in the event that you become victimized in some fashion. If you knew that a criminal was approaching you on the sidewalk, what would you do? Where would you run? Would you fight or faint? Would you start screaming, fighting and running, or would you simply succumb to the wishes of the criminal?

My advice is and always has been this: if confronted by an assailant, and you have reasonable belief that he is going to harm you (and that's a safe bet), then immediately start to scream as loud and as long as is humanly possible. Screaming like this actually gives you strength. Your adrenalin will be off the scales and you can let it work for you. At the same time, run away as fast and as far as possible. If you are going to be raped, you very well may be murdered. This is the time to scream and fight, and run! Even if you believe that the danger has passed, keep it up. Don't be embarrassed; just let it all hang out. The crazier you act — that includes the screaming — the farther away from you the criminal is going to want to be.

You might want to practice this exaggerated screaming, and perhaps some form of fighting and wild gyrations, before you're in a situation like this. It's truly amazing how nuts you can act when you really try, and depending on the circumstances, it can save your life. There are many defensive classes that teach this type of thing; you may want to check with your local police department to see if they offer classes. (If they don't, find out why not!)

If you have done everything right but you still find yourself being robbed, consider throwing bait money. Bait money for our purposes is perhaps a few one-dollar bills secured with an inexpensive, but gaudy-looking money clip. When confronted, pull the bait money out and throw it away from you. The robber will go after the bait money like a rat after cheese. Keep screaming and running. He will want nothing to do with you. Acting a little crazy like this is an excellent tactic that works most of the time. You may be shaken by the experience but at least you will be safe, and the idiot will not have all your money or credit cards.

The Perils of Self Defense

I don't believe that carrying a firearm is necessarily a good idea for some people. Weapons can be taken away from you and used against you. If you have not been thoroughly schooled in the use of a pistol, you should not carry one. A criminal probably knows a great deal more about firearms than you and may be willing to kill you with it.

On the other hand, if you are extremely confident with a pistol, and if you are willing to use it to kill an attacker, carrying a gun may be a good idea. Just know the weapon like it's an extension of your hand, and be ready, willing and able to use it without a moment's hesitation. However, before you purchase a firearm, be sure to check your state and local gun-permitting laws.

If you're carrying mace, throw it away. All that mace will do is to enrage the assailant. As an option, you may want to consider carrying pepper spray, which is usually very effective.

You could consider carrying something like a stun gun, if your state laws allow it. Stun guns have the advantage of creating a psychological effect on the criminal. When he sees 150,000 volts arcing across the two contact points on the stun gun, he may have second thoughts about attacking you. One drawback, of course, is that you have to get within arm's reach of your assailant, and this can put you in great danger. And then there was the man who tried to use a stun gun for self-defense during a robbery, but managed to zap himself. When he woke up his wallet and watch were missing and the robber was nowhere to be seen.

No matter what you may carry for self-defense, remember that the most difficult part is accessing it in time. Crimes occur quickly. You will likely not have enough time to reach inside your handbag to grab the pepper spray or whatever else you think might help, then point it in the right direction and actually hit your target. Studies have shown that even police officers, who are trained to react quickly with deadly force when needed, sometimes do not have enough time to react quickly enough to save their own lives when confronted by an armed assailant. For example, if an assailant is armed with a knife and approaches within about 30 feet of the officer, and the officer has not yet drawn his or her pistol, it is usually too late. From personal experience, having been both shot and stabbed, I can attest to the fact that violence happens very quickly.

Over the years I've had to draw my service weapon countless times. However, I actually used a weapon in my law enforcement work only five times. The first time was many years ago and I was carrying a .38 caliber revolver. I shot off all six rounds, and all six rounds missed. I did quite a lot of damage to the side of a building, but the criminal was unscathed. And I was trained to use the thing! The next four times, however, I made sure there were no court costs that needed to be paid.

So, unless you're actually carrying a weapon ready in your hand, and unless you're willing and able to use it, it's probably a better idea to leave it at home and plan on putting as much space between you and the assailant as possible. If you find yourself the victim of a robbery, let the robber take whatever he wants. This is not the time to be brave. Your life is infinitely more valuable than all of your property. Let the idiot go, but try to remember every detail about him, including the possible direction in which he headed, and the description of any vehicle he used. Immediately call the police (911). Robbers are usually armed.

If you're forced to defend yourself, however, you could use those keys we talked about. If you have several keys on a key ring, they can be carried in your closed fist with the keys sticking out between your fingers, making a wonderful weapon for self-defense. A loud continuous scream and a fist full of keys carried in this manner when directed at the face (the eyes) of the assailant can be very effective in fending off an attacker.

If You Have to Fight

The first few seconds of contact between you and a criminal are most important, and even though you may be frozen with fear, you'd better shake it off and react. It is during those first few seconds that the criminal has the least amount of control over you and the situation. You can take advantage of this and turn things around in your favor. First, remember that screaming, and try to run like mad in the opposite direction.

Although screaming can alert others who may be willing to assist you, don't rely on the good intentions of bystanders to help you. Many of them will keep on walking even when they clearly see that your life is in danger. You may have to fight, and if you do, fight as if you have gone completely insane. Hold absolutely nothing back. Plan to fight as if your life depends on it, because it may.

➢ Aim hard and fast blows to the nose of the criminal. Aim for a point behind the nose, somewhere in the middle of the moron's head. This will increase the chance that you break his nose.

➢ Drive your fists, or the heel of your hands, upwards starting at the base of his nose, above his mouth.

➢ If you're grabbed from behind, use your head to break your assailant's nose.

➢ Start kicking down on top of his feet with all your strength, to try to break the bones on the top of his feet. Aim for a point under his foot (somewhere in the pavement).

➢ Start kicking at the person as if you've become possessed by demons. Go for his genitals. Kick and punch as hard as you can. And keep screaming.

If you're trained in the martial arts, use them. If not, then try the insane mayhem approach. I've used them both, and a few others thrown in for good measure.

You're in good company with this approach. The British equivalent of the American SEAL Team is the elite SAS Commandos known affectionately as "The Regiment." They are taught a form of fighting known as "jap slapping." I don't have the slightest idea where that name originated (probably something left over from World War II), but I do understand the principals involved in this form of fighting. It is meant to be used immediately, within those first few seconds and at the slightest threat, and it is designed to either render harmless or kill an opponent. It entails the most violent form of street fighting in the world. Karate or Tae Kwon Do, or any of the other martial arts are not used. What is used is the most violent tearing of flesh, eye gouging, breaking of bones, genital separation and general mayhem that has ever been known. It is survival fighting, and it works.

I have been a police officer for the better part of my life, and I will tell you that if I'm attacked, my attacker is at the very least going to end up in some emergency room trying to get body parts reattached. I would not lose one moment of sleep over this, either, and neither should you.

If You're Home Alone

If you are home alone or perhaps with your children, and you think that someone is trying to break into your house, then immediately dial 911. Don't wait until you can confirm your suspicions; call the police right away. Police get paid for going after criminals, and I don't know too many officers who wouldn't relish the opportunity to catch a criminal in the act. Studies have shown that a vast majority of people who believe they are about to be victimized hesitate before they pick up the telephone to call for help. It is that momentary hesitation that could get you killed.

➢ If you can safely get out of your house and get to a neighbor's house, call the police from there.

➢ If you can't get out and you believe that someone is definitely breaking into your home, start making noise. Yell out loud as if you're talking with someone. Yell "Richard — I'm going to let the dog out!" The idiot trying to get into your house doesn't know that you don't have a dog, nor does he know that Richard is away or doesn't exist at all.

➢ If everything you have tried does not drive the burglar away, and you've already called the police, arm yourself with something.

➢ Turn all the lights off and hide. Remember, you know the layout of your home far better than the burglar. Even if he does get in he may not be able to find you right away.

➢ Be prepared to fight, scream and run.

The next chapter will give you some specific ideas that can help to keep your home from being burglarized.

To Sum It Up

Any law enforcement officer with a few years of experience will tell you that a great many criminals are similar to predatory animals. Their sole mission in life is to seek out and devour the young, the elderly and the weak, and if the opportunity presents itself they will prey on the rest of us. Predatory animals serve an obvious, useful function. Predatory criminals only serve to make our lives miserable. Criminals place little value on human life. To the predatory criminal, your life is worthless, and if he can somehow take from you, rape or kill you, he will.

The best means of protection is denying criminals access. Do not allow them access to you, your family, your car or your home, or your privacy wherever that might be. Remember:

> ➤ Keep your car doors locked and the windows rolled up.

> ➤ Never give anyone the ability to access your car (remember the lady on the interstate).

> ➤ If you're a female, never get into an elevator if there is a man in it unless you're with others. If you're in an elevator by yourself and a man gets in, simply get out.

> ➤ Whether you're walking alone on a city street, trying to get into an elevator, in your car, at home or anywhere else, be suspicious of others (especially men) and deny them the ability to approach you in any way.

Over thousands of years our survival instincts against predators have been dulled. But we can learn to protect ourselves by practicing to be alert, by having a plan of action, and by not allowing criminals access. The best advice is: use common sense. Your instincts will tell you that something is wrong. Follow those instincts.

It is not my intention to frighten you with this book, but to help you be prepared. If by reading through the following chapters you become just a little more aware and a bit more suspicious, then I have succeeded. In the following pages you will find good, down-to-earth, common-sense approaches in dealing with the criminal element.

Chapter Two

How to Prevent Home Burglaries

According to most sources, a home burglary in the United States occurs approximately every 10 to 12 seconds[7]. And while most burglars are after money, jewelry, DVD players and televisions, they will steal anything they believe they can exchange for cash or drugs. They will also jeopardize your safety and take away your sense of security. Thankfully, using good common sense and thinking like a thief will thwart most burglars. This is what you should know and do.

Think Like a Thief

When it comes to developing strategies to protect your home, it helps to think like a thief. Here are some strategies *they'll* use:

1. "Of course I look familiar, I was just here last week cleaning your carpets, painting your shutters or delivering your brand new refrigerator. You can trust me."
   The moral here? Never trust that guy who comes into your home, ever.

2. "Thanks for letting me use your bathroom when I was working in your yard last week. While I was in there, I unlatched the back window to make my next visit a little easier. You have nothing to worry about"
   Don't trust anyone inside your home, they WILL victimize you.

3. "Oh, I just love those flowers of yours. That tells me you have good taste, and that means there must be nice things in your home. Also, your kids' yard toys make me wonder just what cool gaming systems they have. Keep up the good work."

---

[7] Henderson, Michele and Marshall, Loraine. *Quarterly Review*. Washington, DC: Federal Bureau of Investigation, 2011. Print.

Have a great garden, but just remember what potential burglars look for.

4. "Yes, I really do look for newspapers piled up in your driveway, I sure do. And I just might leave a pizza flyer in your front door to see how long it takes for you to remove it. Once again, you have nothing to worry about, enjoy your time away from home."
ALWAYS keep things neat and tidy, pick everything up, and make it look like there is always someone at home.

5. "I don't take a day off because of bad weather. But that's okay. It's raining and you're fumbling with your keys and your umbrella. That's understandable. And you forgot to lock the front door."
That's NOT understandable. You're asking for trouble.

6. "You don't need to have the snow shoveled."
If it snows while you're out of town, get a neighbor to create car and foot tracks leading to your house. Virgin snow drifts in the driveway are a dead giveaway.

7. "You're so easy, it boggles the mind!"
If decorative glass is part of your front entrance, NEVER let your alarm company install the control pad where a burglar can see whether or not it's set. Alarm your house, yes, but make sure the alarm company follows this suggestion.

8. "Leave your windows alone, really, it's okay."
A good security company alarms the windows over the kitchen sink as well as the windows to the second floor. Those second-story windows oftentimes lead to the master bedroom, and to your jewelry. It's a good idea to put motion detectors up on the second floor as well.

9. "I always knock first. If you answer the door, I'll ask for directions to someplace or offer to clean your gutters, something like that."
DO NOT TAKE HIM UP ON HIS OFFERS! And, by the way, he doesn't always knock first.

10. "I would never look in your sock drawer."

Do you REALLY think he won't look in there? Thieves always check dresser drawers and the bedside table, as well as the medicine cabinet.

11. "I always rummage through the kid's room."
    No they don't. Burglars are in a hurry and, unless they're after your child, will concentrate on the adults' bedrooms and bathrooms.

12. "Oh, come on now, ME?"
    They usually don't have enough time to break into that safe of yours, but if it's not bolted down someplace they'll carry it away.

13. "I love televisions!"
    No they don't. A loud television or a radio can oftentimes be a better deterrent than a good alarm system. But if you're reluctant to leave the television on while you're out of town, you can purchase an inexpensive device that works on a timer and even simulates the flickering glow of a real television. Places like Radio Shack carry them, or how about checking them out at www.faketv.com? Burglars tend to shy away from occupied dwellings, and these devices work quite well at making a potential burglar think your home is occupied.

14. "Leave your lights on at night, and have lots of nightlights on."
    Listen, I know it has something to do with our childhood fears: we just have to have nightlights or other lights on in the house during the hours of darkness. But please, keep them off! Burglars love nightlights. Those cute little nightlights allow criminals to see into your house at night. But you know the layout of your house; the intruder doesn't. Why give the criminal an advantage by keeping lights on in the house?

And in case you have doubts, here are some quotes from actual burglars who have been convicted of their crimes:

1. "Sometimes I carry a clipboard. Sometimes I dress like a lawn guy and carry a rake. I do my best to never, ever look like a crook."

2. "The two things I hate most are loud dogs and nosy neighbors."

3. "I'll break a window to get in, even if it makes a little noise. If your neighbor hears one loud sound, he'll stop what he's doing and wait to hear it again. If he doesn't hear it again, he'll just go back to what he was doing. It's human nature."

4. "I'm not complaining, but why would you pay all that money for a fancy alarm system and leave your house without setting it?"

5. "I love looking in your windows. I'm looking for signs that you're home, and for flat screen TVs or gaming systems I'd like. I'll drive or walk through your neighborhood at night before you close the blinds, just to pick my targets."

6. "Avoid announcing your vacation on your Facebook page. It's easier than you think to look up your address."

7. "To you, leaving that window open just a crack during the day is a way to let in a little fresh air. To me, it's an invitation."

8. "If you don't answer when I knock, I try the door. Occasionally I hit the jackpot and walk right in."

9. "Yeah, houses with lights on at night, or even nightlights, are what I look for."

Act Like a Thief

Now that you know how a thief thinks, try seeing your home the way a thief would see it: try to break in. Yes, you read that right! Have your spouse and children help. Start by leaving, as if you were really leaving. Lock all the doors. Now, try to find a way back in.

Walk around the house looking for an entry point; try everything you can think of. Ask your kids how they would get into the house. Their imaginations have no bounds, and you might be amazed at what they come up with.

You may want to start with the exterior doors of the house, the usual point of entry for a burglar. About 40 percent of burglaries occur through the front door[8].

The back door is also a favorite point of entry. Are there hinges on the outsides of the doors? Could you remove them to gain entry? Could the door be kicked in easily? Can the lock be picked? If you have sliding glass doors, see if you can get them open.

If your home has an attached garage, try to gain entry through the garage.

Next, try the first-floor windows. If you can approach a window on the first floor, you can probably get inside. If you (or a burglar) can stand outside of your home and place your hands on the window, there's a good chance you (or the burglar!) will get in. If a window is unlocked, entry will be easy. (But if it's locked, a burglar could just as easily break the glass.)

If you haven't been able to get into your home yet, try the basement windows. Are they readily accessible? Could they be kicked in easily?

If you're still unable to break in, congratulations. You are well on your way to creating a safe and secure environment. But if you've discovered potential entry points, here are some things you can do:

> Replace exterior doors that do not have a solid core or are not made of metal, including any doors that lead to the house from an attached garage.

> Make sure exterior doors are hinged on the inside.

> Make sure all exterior doors (including the garage door) have adequate locks.

> Make the approaches to first-floor windows as difficult or as uncomfortable as possible. (You could plant thorny rosebushes under the windows, or if you live in a warm climate, plant thorny cacti.)

> Consider adding security bars to your first-floor windows. Without making your home look like an armed camp,

---

[8] United States. *Quarterly Review*. Washington, DC: Federal Bureau of Investigation, 2011. Print.

security bars can add both beauty and safety. (A word of caution: If you do decide to use security bars, remember to install the types that can be opened easily from the inside, in case of a fire. Manufacturers now make designer burglar bars that have simple push-button opening mechanisms.)

➢ If your basement windows have lightweight latches on the inside, they should be replaced. You might consider having the basement windows secured with metal bars as well.

➢ About those sliding glass doors, or "sliders" as we have come to know them: First, know that they are loved by burglars. As you may have discovered, they can be opened pretty easily. Even if the door is locked, all one has to do is to lift it up and pull outwards. This is usually sufficient to take the door right out of its tracks. There are a few inexpensive mechanisms on the market that make it more difficult for burglars, and they are well worth the small investment, such as track bars, auxiliary track locks and locking pins.

➢ You may want to consider replacing your sliding doors with French doors that have safety glass. The French doors have better locks, are much harder to break into and, in my humble opinion, are better looking.

You should remember that burglars do not want to be inconvenienced or hurt, and they don't want to be seen or heard. They just want to get in relatively easily, steal what they can, and get away. Anything that you and I can do to screw their plans up is really okay.

Fortify Your House

Alarms

The obvious thing to do to protect your home is to get an alarm system, complete with motion detectors and a loud siren. The system should connect directly to your police department, not to the alarm company operators. An alarm system can be expensive and at times inconvenient, but it does give you some piece of mind. And although it will not stop all burglars, it will stop most of them. In a recent University of Miami study, more than 90 percent of convicted burglars said they would avoid breaking into a home with an alarm system[9]. If you have a system installed, make sure that all of the first-floor windows and doors are covered by the system, as well as the basement windows.

If an alarm system is just not viable for you at the moment, you can still purchase two or three of those metal alarm company signs directly from the companies and display alarm security systems decals on your doors and windows. They have an amazing deterrent effect: the burglar is unlikely to realize there isn't actually an alarm installed.

Locks

Make sure all your exterior doors have very good locks. Strong and effective dead-bolt locks, when added to keyed entryways, enhance security. *Remember, they must be dead-bolt locks.* Dead-bolts should have a minimum of a 1-inch throw, meaning that the bolt extends a minimum of 1 inch. My personal recommendation is that the dead-bolt should have about a 2-inch bolt. In addition, the lock itself should be equipped with cylinder guards in order to prevent tampering. The locking mechanism should have interlocking chassis and reinforced, extra-large strike plates.

As an extra precaution, you might consider adding double-cylinder dead-bolts that require keys to operate from both sides. (However, if you do this, make sure that the key for the interior lock is easily accessible, in the event of a fire in the house.) You can leave the key in the interior lock if there isn't any glass in the door and if there isn't a window within about 40 inches of the lock. This will prevent intruders from reaching in for the key, even if they can't get their bodies through the opening.

The locks and mechanisms that you buy will come with a set of screws for ease of installation. My advice is to set those screws aside and buy screws that are twice as long. One of the weakest links in home security is the marginal screws that come with locks and door plates. You might want to consider replacing all of the screws in and around your doors — a simple and inexpensive measure that adds

---

[9] Marshall, Anthony G. *Top 500 Chains Report*. Florida International University, Miami: School of Hospitality Management, 2006. Print.

significantly to safety.

Finally, remember to change all of the locks when you move into a new house or apartment. There could be a chance that a former owner or tenant might still have keys to your home.

Structural Precautions

It might be a good idea to use peepholes in all of your exterior doors, even the ones leading to the backyard. These will help you get a look at whoever might be at the door before you decide to let him in. Some people use small door chains as a way to get a quick look at who's at the door. Don't waste your time on those. As far as I'm concerned, door chains are completely useless. They can be easily broken by someone pushing on the door. Don't use them — use the peepholes instead.

You should also consider replacing the door jambs on your exterior doors. (Those are the two sidepieces for the door frame.) Most contractors install the least expensive, least sturdy kinds of door jambs. Some are little more than decorative features and can be easily pried away. Most burglars don't use a great deal of finesse when it comes to breaking into a house. Many will simply try to kick a door in. A strong, well-built door jamb will keep that from happening.

Keep It Secure

Law enforcement agencies across the country report that burglars often simply access houses through unlocked doors and windows. It may sound elementary, but the first rule to follow when you leave your house — even for just a few minutes — is to lock all of your doors and windows. There are inexpensive devices on the market that enhance the security of windows, and even allow the windows to be opened a few inches without allowing access to the inside. And don't forget to lock the garage door. I have lost count of how many times thieves have gained entry to homes through open garage doors while the owners simply went to the corner grocery store or were working or sunbathing in the backyard.

When it comes to keys, be wary of giving out any keys to your home. If you must, give keys to only a few trusted people. Do not leave spare keys in obvious places such as door mats, mailboxes, flower pots and above the doors themselves. Burglars may be morons, but they're not that stupid; they actually do look in those places.

Be extremely careful about allowing a valet car attendant access to your keys. This also applies to automobile service shops and garages. Allow those people access to only the ignition key. Some keys, such as house keys, may have identifying tags, which can provide a thief with personal information, such as your name and address. Purchase a separate key ring for your house keys, and keep those keys separate from your car keys. Remember, keys can be duplicated in a very short amount of time. Anyone with access to your house keys and your car registration, which most people keep inside the car's glove box, can easily find your address and pay a visit to your home with the new key.

Strategies for Protecting Your Home

Protect Identifying Information

Thieves look for identifying information wherever they can find it, including your mailbox. It's a good idea not to have your name displayed on your mailbox or your house; display the house numbers only. If a thief knows your name and address, he can simply look up your telephone number in the phone book and then call the number to see if you're home.

As a matter of safety, your house number should be prominently displayed and easily seen, and should be made of reflective material so it can be seen at night. If you were to call the police, fire department or paramedics in an emergency, the last thing you would want is for the responders to be frantically searching up and down the street trying to locate your house. An excellent idea for a community or neighborhood project is to have the house numbers painted directly on the curbing in front of each residence, if local ordinances allow. If there is an ordinance prohibiting the painting of numbers on the curbing, you could work with your neighbors to get it changed.

Beware of Strangers

No matter what, never allow anyone into your home unless you are absolutely comfortable with them. Remember, once you let a stranger into your house, you've lost control of the situation. Don't let them in; do call the police.

The Guises They Use to Get In

Thieves often pose as salespeople, repairmen, or lost travelers asking to use a telephone. Tell unsolicited salespeople to leave their business cards or brochures in the mailbox or on the front steps. You can always call them back at another time if you're interested in what they're selling.

Sometimes would-be thieves claim to be having an emergency and may come to your door seeking help. If that's the case, dial 911, but don't let them in.

If someone purporting to be a service representative comes to your door, ask for identification, but don't let him in. Have him hold the identification up in front of the peephole. Call the company he says he works for, or better yet, call the police. Whatever you do, don't let him in.

Some criminals often try to impersonate police officers. If someone claiming to be an officer comes to your door, ask the "officer" to show his badge and identification. A badge is sometimes easy to acquire, but real identification is not. Call the police department to verify his identity. If it's a real officer waiting outside, he won't mind.

What to do About Uninvited Visitors

Be very careful of anyone paying you a visit when you haven't personally invited him. If someone knocks on the door or rings your doorbell, don't ignore it—that would be like telling someone you're not at home. Answer the door verbally, but don't open it. Use that peephole. And just because the man at your door looks like he's a gentleman, it doesn't mean he is.

Dealing with Contractors

If you have arranged to have work done inside your house, make sure that all of your valuable items—including money, credit cards, jewelry, prescription drugs and important documents, etc.—are locked safely away.

Do not allow anyone free rein inside your home, and do not remain home alone with anyone unfamiliar working inside your house. Have a friend by your side, or have your spouse take a day off from work. At the very least, make sure that you stay on the telephone with a friend while the worker is inside your house.

When contractors complete work at your house, do an inventory check. If anything is missing call the police right away. Also, you should check that your telephone, security alarm systems and electrical circuits are up and running. Things can get damaged because of the contractor's work crew. And wires can be cut intentionally.

I remember conducting a home security check for a young couple who just bought a new townhouse in Florida. During the course of my detailed inspection, I pulled out the inner panel to a wall-mounted air-conditioning unit, and found a brand new house key at the base of the unit, which was also accessible from the exterior of the home.

After my inspection, we conducted an investigation and found that the subcontractor who installed the air-conditioning units for all the townhouses in the area did his work at the same time that the door locks were being installed. He simply helped himself to a key for each townhouse and placed the keys at the bottom of the air conditioners. It doesn't take a genius to know what was going through his brain. In all, 117 keys were found in 117 townhouses. I couldn't arrest the contractor for this (not enough proof or evidence of a crime, according to the attorney general's office), but managed to get him on something else, thank you very much!

Use caution in hiring lawn maintenance firms. Many, if not most, of those employees are not given any sort of background checks. Some lawn-care companies have been known to employ people with pretty lengthy criminal histories. Be careful about what company you hire.

Finally, beware of sharing information about your schedule with people like contractors during the course of casual conversations. Remember that it can become easy to let your guard down with workers you see every day, and use caution.

Beware of Gypsies—Really!

Believe it or not, thousands of gypsy families live right here in the United States. Most of them are fine, upstanding individuals, but many follow in the footsteps of their ancestors committing a variety of crimes, including residential burglaries. Some run scams, such as instant driveway and roof repair. Many gypsies drive newer-model pickup trucks with camper tops. I don't have anything against gypsies or anyone else (even though an elderly gypsy woman once gave cursed me with "fire from the moon"). I just think it's a good idea to be very suspicious of people who look like they just don't belong in the area. Your instincts will guide you. Pay attention to those uneasy feelings.

Use a Vacation Checklist

If you decide to take a vacation, use the following 10-step checklist to help keep your home secure while you're away.

1. Do not be overly communicative about your vacation plans. (Don't post your plans on Facebook!)

2. Don't let automated messages on your e-mail account or telephone reveal your vacation plans. Make sure that your telephone answering messages don't say you are not at home. Erase your incoming messages often. This can be done remotely, which makes it less obvious that you are away. Do use an answering machine or voice mail, but don't allow the telephone to ring constantly as if there is no one at home.

3. Use timers on lights, radios and televisions. Use timers with random patterns. This suggests movement and activity within the house.

4. Ask the police to check your property often. They may ask you to fill out a simple one-page Vacation House Check form, which is pretty standard practice. But what isn't standard is for you to request a copy of the log of those house checks, although you are, indeed, entitled to a copy of this. Requesting one will ensure that your house gets checked frequently. You can pick it up from the police department when you return.

5. Secure all of the locks on the doors and windows. This includes the garage, shed, and even the pet door. (It's amazing what some people can squeeze through just to steal someone else's property!) Don't forget to set the house alarms if you have them, and don't forget to fill up that large dog bowl with water (the one by the back door).

6. Use lighting and electronics to deter thieves. Replace old light bulbs with new, high-quality, long-lasting bulbs. Consider using a couple of those neat devices that emulate a television playing. If you have lights on timers, vary the times at which the lights are activated. If they go on and off at exactly the same time each night, even a dim-witted burglar who may have been watching your house for a while would realize that no one is home.

7. Make arrangements to have your yard maintained. This includes having the lawn mowed on a regular basis, or the snow shoveled.

8. Have someone you trust pick up your mail and newspaper every day. Do not let the newspaper company or the post office know that you will be away.

9. Don't close all the shades and curtains. That would be much too obvious to a thief.

10. Leave a car in the driveway and have your trusted friend move it about a little each day. You could have your neighbor park his car in your driveway while you're away. Have him bring a bag or two of his trash for deposit in your trash can, and have him bring the trash can to your curb for pick-up.

Know Your Neighborhood; Enlist Their Support

First, before buying property anywhere, call the local police department to find out the frequency of burglaries or any criminal activity in the area and how they occurred. You are allowed to have this kind of information, and it may help you develop strategies to protect your home.

When you move to a new neighborhood, familiarize yourself with the physical details of the area, the people and the activities. Then, get to know your neighbors. You and your neighbors will often know who should or should not be in the area.

Ask your police department how to go about forming a Neighborhood Watch. A Neighborhood Watch is a group of citizens organized to help prevent crime and vandalism in their neighborhood, with support from the police. Most law enforcement agencies have Neighborhood Watch programs and have the personnel to assist you with whatever you need in getting one started in your neighborhood. They'll likely be more than happy to help. Some police departments may need a little encouragement, but, being accountable to the local town officials, mayors or city managers, they will eventually do whatever it takes to assist you. Neighborhood Watch programs are free to you and the city, and studies have shown that when Neighborhood Watch signs are posted at the entrances to subdivisions, there is usually a marked decrease in the incidence of criminal activity in the area. Participants in a Neighborhood Watch take note of all suspicious strangers, including their descriptions and procedures, and alert each other as well as the police.

Other Home Protection Ideas

➤ *Get a dog.* I have interviewed many burglars over the years, and most of them told me that the one thing that deters them from breaking into a house is knowing that there is a dog in the home or on the property somewhere. Dogs not only frighten intruders, but also warn you with their barking. And ultimately they may protect you. I have a corgi that weighs about 25 pounds, but her ears are like radar antennas, and her bark is like a shot of lightning right through your head. She wouldn't actually harm anyone, but a burglar wouldn't know that.

➤ *Get a dog bowl.* If you don't want a dog, place a large dog bowl conspicuously outside of your back door or somewhere inside of the house where it can be easily seen by someone looking in. Let burglars think there's a 120-pound German Shepherd waiting for them inside.

➤ *Get "beware of the dog" signs,* or an alarm that sounds like a dog barking. Both work quite well in deterring burglars.

➤ *Use motion-detecting lighting around your property.* This type of lighting is relatively inexpensive, but well worth it. (Thieves hate motion–detectors!) The lights should be located out of reach. It's not unusual for a burglar to simply remove a light bulb, so a good rule of thumb would be to have all the exterior motion-sensitive lights mounted at least 9 feet off of the ground. (And these types of lights can be adjusted so that the neighborhood cat doesn't constantly set them off.)

➢ *Try to keep the trees and shrubs around your house trimmed back.* If you are unable to clearly see your front door from the street, trim back whatever is blocking your line of sight. Overgrown trees and shrubs not only mask the activities of a thief, but can also be used by prowlers to look through your windows at night. This is more common than you may realize.

➢ *Remove trees or branches that are close to your house* and could afford burglars access to the second-floor windows.

➢ *Keep your lawn and garden well-maintained* to let thieves know your house is properly attended-to and lived-in. They will go somewhere else.

➢ *Make sure there are adequate locks on fence gates.* Remember that burglars don't want to be seen, and they love fenced-in backyards for that reason! The best kinds of gates and fences have spikes on top, or other components that dissuade burglars from climbing over.

➢ *Don't keep ladders or tools lying around the outside of your house.* Thieves are great opportunists and will make excellent use out of every available resource, such as a ladder, to get to the second floor. Keep your yard cleaned up, and store tools in a locked garage or shed.

➢ *Keep your neighbors informed.* Let trusted neighbors know when you'll be having work done on your home, and when you plan to be away. That will keep them on alert so they can immediately report to the police any suspicious activity at your home.

➤ *Set up your entryways for safety.* If you enter your house though a door other than an interior garage door, such as the front or side door, you may want to consider having a convenient table or bench just inside the door. That way, if you have your hands full of packages or briefcases, you can put them down right away and lock the door behind you. If you drive into the garage, use the garage door opener to shut the door behind you before getting out of the car.

➤ *Consider checking on your elderly relatives and friends* as often as possible, and also make sure that their security devices and smoke/fire detectors are functioning properly.

Protect Yourself from Intruders

In the unlikely event that you return home to find someone inside your house, do not go inside, but instead go immediately to a neighbor's house and call the police. Use a cell phone, if you have one. But, if you have to defend yourself, here are some things you can do:

➤ If you don't carry a firearm, use wasp spray; that stuff is great. A receptionist in a church located in a high crime area asked the local police department whether or not they'd recommend pepper spray. They said wasp spray was better, because a can of wasp spray can shoot up to and beyond 20 feet and is much more accurate than the pepper spray. (I tested a can and it shot out accurately to just over 32 feet.) Aimed at the eyes of an intruder, it is devastating. With pepper spray, you have to be no more than 8 or 10 feet away from the criminal — and that's way too close. That receptionist now keeps a can of wasp spray on her desk at all times, and it doesn't attract attention like a can of pepper spray would. She also keeps a can of wasp spray in her home, just in case.

➤ Keep your car keys beside your bed at night. If you hear a noise or think that someone is trying to break into your house, just press the panic button on your car key ring. The car alarm will be set off, and the horn will continue to sound until you either turn it off or the car battery dies. The panic button will set off that car alarm from just about anywhere in your house. Think of it as a free security alarm system. Whether your car is parked in the garage or in your driveway, this works, and it will frighten off the intruder. They don't want to be heard, and they'll run away. Remember to call 911 immediately — don't wait a second.

➤ A good idea, especially for the elderly, is to carry car keys in a pocket. If the person falls and is unable to get up, or becomes disabled in some other way, he could push that panic alarm for the car, which could quickly attract help.

Chapter Three

Business Security

Some of the simple ideas from the last chapter can be used in your business to help create a secure environment for your workplace and your employees.

You should be aware of the times when your business is the most at risk for burglary or other crimes. Those times are as follows:

1. The time immediately following the firing of an employee.

2. When there are multiple sets of keys in circulation.

3. When you and your employees have a consistent schedule.

4. Just after you move your business to a new location.

5. When you take extended vacations.

Beware Disgruntled Employees

Studies and my personal experience have shown that disgruntled former employees, or employees who have been recently fired or laid off from their jobs, pose a great risk to businesses. Investigators looking into the burglary of a business almost always have to check the possibility that a former employee, or perhaps one who had a disagreement with a supervisor, could be involved with the crime. Once an employer has identified the potential for a problem with a former employee, he should take definitive steps ensure that the business is protected against potential acts of revenge. This may include changing the locks.

I know of one notorious law enforcement agency in Florida where all of the entrances into the building utilize combination locks. The chief of police and the patrol commander of this agency were so corrupt and overly harsh in their treatment of employees that many fine officers and civilian personnel left in disgust. Every time this happened the chief would have all of the combinations to the locks changed. It was actually a standing joke in the local law enforcement community. You could always tell when someone had resigned; officers would come to work and not be able to get into the building.

Protect Keys and Locks

It should be standard practice to limit the number of keys that are in circulation at your business. Certain employees and maintenance personnel will need to have keys, but the keys should be tightly controlled and monitored. It is actually a very good idea to have all of the locks and keys changed at least a couple of times a year. This is an expense and an inconvenience, but it is a good control mechanism and cuts down on the number of keys in circulation.

Remember that locks are your first line of defense. The locks you choose for your business should have patented key controls to guard against unauthorized key duplication. The locks should also be the type that are resistant to picking and drilling. Combination locks may not be the best choice for your business, since they do not offer a high level of security. With standard access systems, such as those key pads, anyone watching you or an employee enter a passcode gains instant "duplicated keys" that can be used at any time. I have seen this many times at airports, for example, where pilots, flight attendants or agents punch in a small series of numbers to access the jet way leading to an airplane.

Keep an Unpredictable Schedule

One issue that could pose a risk to business security is a consistent schedule. As an example, if you were to open your business every Monday through Friday at 8:00 a.m. and close at 5:00 p.m., and consistently have every weekend off, then even the dumbest criminal would soon know your routine. It would then be relatively easy to plan the time of a crime. If at all possible, establish a schedule with varying hours of operation.

When the criminal sees that your business is operating some evenings or early mornings or weekends, it becomes a complication for him, making it likely that he will choose to look at someone else's business. I have interviewed scores of criminals, including burglars, and the constant refrain I hear is that they want it to be "easy and quick." So whatever you do to complicate his life is good.

Take Precautions After a Move

Another problem that businesses often face is the situation where the business itself is being relocated. Criminals know that when a new business has just opened or has just moved into a new location, the alarms are probably not in place, or perhaps all of the locks are not yet installed. Whatever the I.Q. of the criminal may or may not be, he probably knows that the newly opened business is an easier and more attractive target than all the other established businesses that have their alarms and locks in good working order.

Make sure not to move your valuable items, such as computers, electronic components and records, etc., into the new business location until those alarms and locks are up and running.

Finally, you might want to consider hiring a security guard for an abbreviated period of time after a move, but at the very least, let the local police department know of your situation. They can provide extra patrols of the area.

Thieves Don't Take Vacations

If you're in the habit of taking extended vacations away from your business, you must be certain that whoever is left in charge while you're away is well trusted and understands all of the security needs. There are many documented cases where employees have taken advantage of the fact that their employer is away. Not only do burglaries and thefts occur, but the quality of the work being done by some employees can drop off dramatically.

If you actually close your business and leave for vacation, make sure that someone is monitoring all the alarms, locks and general security each day. Let the police know that your business is temporarily closed.

Improve Building Security

The best way to help protect your business is to keep the building itself as secure as possible. Follow this checklist to ensure your building's physical security:

> ➢ Use metal or solid core doors.

> Attach sheet steel to both sides of basement and back doors.

> Use tamper-resistant door frames and hinges.

> Use high-security padlocks on steel bars and door barriers. The padlocks should have hardened steel bodies and shackles that are resistant to bolt cutters, drills, acetylene torches and hammers.

> Secure all the windows.

> Ensure that the fire escapes do not provide easy access to upper levels of the building.

> Make sure there is a clear view into and out of your business is best. Trees and bushes should be trimmed on a regular basis.

> Install motion-sensitive lighting inside the building and constant lighting on the outside. As with my earlier advice on home security, have the exterior lighting installed at least 9 feet off of the ground.

> Keep interior lights on when the business is closed, to give police patrols a clear view inside at night. The lighting should be installed to reflect silhouettes to the exterior of the business. (You could simply have some of the lights placed in the rear of the rooms.)

> Eliminate shadows and dark areas around your building at night, to help remove hiding places.

Protect Valuables

If you have a safe on the premises, you should have it positioned in clear view to the outside, but securely bolted to the floor (unless, of course, you have it safely hidden away in some sort of James Bond setup). This may go against your instincts, but remember that while the thief may see the safe, he is usually not so stupid as to attempt to break into it or remove it. He does not want to be seen, heard or inconvenienced in any way.

The key or combination to the safe should only be available to trusted and authorized personnel. Here are some other "safe" precautions:

> The combination code should be changed frequently.

> Ensure that the dials on the safe are turned several after the vault is closed, to be certain that it is completely locked.

> Make frequent bank deposits to ensure that a minimum amount of cash is stored in your business. Deposits should not be on a regular schedule, but should be made at varying times of the day.

> Post a sign prominently, indicating that only small amounts of cash—or none at all—are kept on hand at your business.

> Request an escort for bank deposits. Most law enforcement agencies are more than happy to provide you with an escort. However, if you do not have an escort, vary your route to the bank.

Train Employees to be Alert

Another important aspect of keeping your business secure is having proper security procedures in place and training your employees. Here are some good rules to follow:

> All visitors to your business should be escorted by a designated employee. Never allow people other than employees to have free movement within your business.

> As in retail operations, be wary of people wearing bulking coats or outer garments, or carrying large bags, parcels and even umbrellas. Thieves hide things everywhere.

> Train employees to be thoroughly familiar with positive identification of credit-card holders. They should also be

very familiar with spotting counterfeit money and suspicious checks.

> Train employees to be on the lookout for suspicious activity. Have them report any suspicious activity in or around your business. Ask them to remember the physical features of suspicious people and immediately write down any detailed descriptions — of suspicious people or events — before the memory fades. They should also try to record the license plate number of any vehicle used in suspicious activity. Finally, make sure they know when to call the police.

Every business is different, and each has its own unique requirements for security. A business owner's responsibility should be to make the environment as secure as possible. This list, if used as a guide, will help ensure that your business will not be victimized.

Chapter Four

Corporate Security

According to Justice Department and police figures, it is estimated that 40 to 45 percent of the nearly 40,000 businesses that fail each year do so because of employee theft[10]. We are a trusting lot. People in my generation, and most certainly the generation before me, actually trust that people are inherently honest, and that in a business environment people will work hard and try to enhance the image and the profit margin for the company. Unfortunately this is not always the case:

A company vice president may give too much responsibility to an assistant, who secretly makes unauthorized personal purchases with corporate funds. A human resources manager may unknowingly hire a dock worker who has a history of fraudulent worker's compensation claims. The chief executive officer may dismiss the seriousness of a potential labor strike that suddenly turns violent. A supervisor may turn a blind eye to employees that leave the premises each day without authorization to purchase and distribute cocaine.

If any of these scenarios sounds familiar to you, it is not surprising. We, by and large, tend to trust others. We have to be somewhat trusting, because without trust we couldn't possibly conduct our businesses. But we must be suspicious of others in our business relationships as well as in our personal lives.

Screen Employees

Because of the trust companies must place in their employees, it's most important that they know who they're hiring. Trying to find the right employee for any job must go far beyond simply checking into an applicant's past performance or assessing his ability to properly handle the job's requirements. Many companies have been accused of negligent hiring simply because they failed in some way to carefully check an applicant's background before he was hired. Some untoward

---

[10] United States. Department of Justice. *Quarterly Review*. Washington, DC: Bureau of Justice Standards, 2010. Print.

action by an employee, such as theft, robbery, wrongful death or sexual assault, could force a company to spend thousands of dollars in legal expenses. This could also create adverse publicity and impact the company's credibility.

Aside from helping to avoid a negligent hiring lawsuit, selecting the right employee can have a positive tangible impact on the company's profit margin and reap other benefits, such as:

> Reducing internal losses and theft.

> Producing higher worker productivity, with fewer absences and discipline problems.

> Encouraging better performance from employees, and creating higher morale.

> Reducing the employee turnover rate, which would reduce costs associated with hiring and training, as well as FICA taxes.

> Reducing insurance costs, including medical premiums and worker's compensation claims.

There are a number of methods available to check a potential employee's background during the pre-employment screening process. Here are some of the more popular methods:

> *Criminal history check.* The failure to obtain adequate criminal history information is one of the most common reasons for employer liability, according to J. Stewart MacDonald, PhD, an international corporate security consultant. The law enforcement agency in your area can conduct these checks either free of charge or for a token fee. The criminal history will include convictions for theft, drug use, drunk driving and any other felony or misdemeanor crime. The criminal history check should also indicate the person's arrest record, as well as the conviction record.

> *Driving records check.* According to Dr. MacDonald, an applicant's driving history will determine the validity of the actual driver's license and will show any traffic

citations. This process can single out individuals with serious or multiple violations. That information is especially critical if the applicant is to drive a company vehicle.

> *Credit history check.* In an address to Heriot-Watt University, Dr. MacDonald said that a credit history check will show an applicant's financial credit record, payment patterns, and any liens against him[11]. This, in turn, can be an indicator of his character. The information is most useful if the applicant is to be considered for positions dealing with budgets, accounting, upper-level management or any other position that have responsibility for money.

> *Drug screening.* Testing for the use of unlawful drugs should be in place for all employees and a standard written policy should be in effect. The written policy will have the effect of thwarting possible harassment or discrimination practice claims against the company.

> *Employment history check.* Dr. MacDonald has said that fully 25 to 30 percent of résumés contain false or misleading information. Résumés should be thoroughly checked for accuracy, and job performance ratings should be reviewed.

> *Workers' compensation check.* A percentage of all workers' compensation and injury claims are completely false or exaggerated, so any worker's compensation claims made by an applicant should be reviewed.

> *Honesty test.* According to the Survey on Workplace Testing, by the American Management Research Association, "Paper-and-pencil honesty tests are administered by 30 percent of the companies in the retail and wholesale industry, where employee theft is the highest.[12]" The validity of these tests should be checked,

---

[11] Dr. J. Stewart MacDonald. Security Seminar. Heriot-Watt University, Edinburg, Scotland, 2010.

[12] United States. Department of Labor. *Survey on Workplace Testing.* Washington, DC: American Management Association Research. 2002. Print.

and they must absolutely adhere to the guidelines of the Equal Employment Opportunity Commission as well as the Standards for Educational and Psychological Testing of the American Psychological Association[13][14]. Employers are cautioned to keep an open mind when it comes to these honesty tests, as they are extremely subjective in nature.

➤ *Psychological test.* Sometimes referred to as a personality test, a psychological test can be an indicator of one's aptitude, knowledge and skill, and can provide insight into a person's personality and behavior. However, the American Disabilities Act of 1990 says that employers cannot refuse to hire an applicant because of a physical or mental ailment.

There are some states, and Florida is one of them, that have Subsequent Injury Trust Funds in order to assist employers with certain costs associated with these screening tools. If, as an example, the employer hires someone who has had previous workers' compensation claims, the fund will pay a percentage, or in some cases all, of the subsequent injuries.

One important thing to remember regarding all of this is the need for accurate documentation. No matter which tests are used to screen potential applicants, documentation of all the information is paramount in order to avoid negligent hiring liability. Such litigations are not normally resolved for years after an employee has been hired. Therefore, documentation is absolutely crucial.

Remember also that you must be consistent in your actions. For example, if the decision is made to conduct a criminal history check and perhaps a drug screening for a position at risk, then the tests must be administered to *all* of the applicants for that position.

I suggest that every company assesses each and every position for potential liability claims. Upper-level managers are not the only ones who require screening. Employee theft, and other untoward activity, surfaces on all steps of the company ladder.

---

[13] Shoemaker, Karen. *Annual Report.* Washington, DC: The Equal Employment Opportunity Commission. 2009. Print.

[14] Litlowe, Jason and Rheimes, Claudia. *Standards for Educational and Psychological Testing.* Washington, DC: American Psychological Association. 2009. Print.

Protect Against Drug-Related Losses

Theft and some of those other crimes are not the only problems that plague businesses. According to the National Institute on Drug Abuse in a report to Congress, one in fourteen employees abuse drugs on the job[15]. Drug abuse is now seen as one of the leading health-related issues in the work place. Illnesses and absences directly stemming from illegal drug use now translate to an estimated $125 billion in lost productivity each year. And that figure is steadily on the rise, no matter what politicians may want you to believe. Drug use is also a factor in employee theft: people steal from others to support their addictions. No matter where a company is located, if there are ten employees using drugs while working, the chances are that three of them are actively stealing.

The National Institute on Drug Abuse points to the very real possibility that some businesses will become so adversely affected in a few years that unless the trend is somehow turned around, the primary concern will not be the product line or the competition, but instead the ability to actually stay in business, with an ever-increasing number of employees using drugs on a daily basis.

Not long ago, I accompanied an Italian police officer to a small fish-processing center in the town of Portogruaro, located on the northern coast of the Adriatic Sea. A complaint had been filed by the owner of the company, stating that several of his employees were at times openly using alcohol and drugs, and that money and commercial fishing gear were being stolen from his business. The police officer related how the two problems of theft and drug or alcohol abuse go hand in hand, and said that she has seen an alarming increase in these cases in the last five years. (Thanks to her dedication and hard work, all of the employees involved in the thefts were placed under arrest, and all but one were convicted in court. She recently told me that the business owner has not had a repeat of the problems he faced, has seen his profit margin increase dramatically and has even earned a reputation in the local community as a firm, yet fair employer.)

By far, the vast majority of drug abuse and drug trafficking occurs in distribution centers or warehouse environments, but don't think for a moment that the problem is limited to the blue collar worker. A recent survey conducted by the National Cocaine Hotline of

---

[15] Volkow, Nora, MD. *Congressional Report for Illicit and Prescription Drug Abuse*. Washington, DC: National Institute on Drug Abuse, 2010. Print.

drug users found that with an average 19 percent of those with an annual salary of $83,000 were dealing cocaine, and 18 percent of cocaine abusers were stealing from their employers.

Employers should be on the lookout for warning signs about drug abuse on the job, including:

> Nonemployee traffic in the parking lot or lounge areas

> An increase in the number of employee theft cases

> A rise in the numbers of workers' compensation claims. (The National Institute on Drug Abuse has stated that drug users are "five times more likely than nonusers to file claims.")

> High rates of absenteeism

> Poor quality control.

Takes Steps to Prevent Employee Theft

It's just not the drug users who are stealing from corporations. Others, from upper-level management to clerical personnel, are also responsible for the increases in embezzlement, fraud, kickbacks and bribery—crimes that go unnoticed most of the time. In my opinion, the primary reason that employees get away with these crimes is that high-level management is often too busy to conduct thorough audits, too unsuspecting of thieving employees, or perhaps simply unaware of how to control the problems. These are some steps corporations can take to dissuade employee theft:

1. Conduct thorough pre-employment background checks on all potential employees, such as credit and criminal history checks, reference investigations, drug screening and past employment checks.

2. Implement a companywide drug-testing program.

3. Implement a hotline so that employees can anonymously report internal theft or drug-use occurrences.

4. Conduct random register checks on cashiers in order to verify accurate sales totals.

5. Document and cross-check all incoming shipments.

6. Record on videotape the loading and unloading of delivery trucks.

7. Use an outside management specialist to periodically verify inventories.

There are other steps that can be taken if drug use, theft and fraud are discovered to be a problem in your company:

➤ *Implement the use of undercover operatives.* There are times when this is the only viable way to determine the extent of the problem, as well as to identify the people involved in the criminal activity. Some security companies offer this type of service, but it can be quite costly, because most undercover operations will take a minimum of two to three months. Some law enforcement agencies have officers working in special investigations units that will be happy to assist in most instances. If you do decide to initiate this type of investigation, take steps to prevent litigation against your company. Make sure that:

1. All suspects have been interviewed and have had a chance to complete written affidavits relating to their activity.

2. Loss control programs have been started.

3. Comprehensive drug policies and preventive drug programs have been initiated.

4. An employee incentive award program has been put in place.

➤ *Conduct audits.* This can help uncover internal paperwork frauds and can identify employees who might be receiving kickbacks from vendors, as well as purchasing agents who might be setting up fictitious vendors.

> *Use outside surveillance cameras.* If a company has reason to believe that merchandise is being removed by employees in a specific area, the actual theft can be recorded on videotape for prosecution or disciplinary action. An agent or a police officer can be used for this investigation.

> *Use covert cameras.* In addition to using highly visible security cameras, which have proven useful in slowing down the instances of criminal activity, you may decide to use any of a wide variety of covert cameras. Some of these cameras are about the size of a matchbook and can be concealed quite easily. They have excellent track records for finding the perpetrators of theft and other crimes. If merchandise is believed to be going out of a certain warehouse door, a covert camera can be installed to cover the exit. You could also position a camera over a work station in order to document any transactions. This is not an infringement on a person's right to privacy, but instead is an outstanding tool that can be used by businesses to check on the activities of the employees. Cameras cannot be used in areas such as bathrooms or locker rooms where there is indeed an expectation of privacy. But in the general workplace they are most appropriate.

Covert cameras are the most cost-effective method for catching dishonest employees. But if you use them, be careful. I know of a retail chain of stores that followed that bit of advice with great success. And then they caught a female cashier pocketing some money from the cash drawer. When confronted with the evidence (the video tape), the cashier asked to see the tape. When she saw herself putting the money into her handbag, she immediately accused the store manager of having people look down her blouse! And believe it or not, she won her case against the store. The bad luck for the store that day was the fact that she was wearing a loose-fitting blouse, which did reveal quite a lot to that camera. That, and the fact that they allowed her to see the tape in the first place, was wrong. They should have waited until it was subpoenaed by her attorney (which may never have happened). So, where should the camera have been placed? Well, perhaps not directly over her head, but at least at enough of an acute angle to get a clear picture of the work station, without revealing anything else. The female employee did have a legitimate issue regarding this matter. She was indeed a thief, but her privacy had been violated.

Prevent Workers' Comp Fraud

In 1996, the Georgia State Board of Worker's Compensation reported that corporations spent about $300 million annually on fraudulent claims, with about $7,700 spent on each claim[16]. That figure has risen dramatically since then, not only Georgia, but also in many other states. In fact, fraudulent workers' compensation claims are taking a toll on companies nationwide.

Companies can decrease the numbers of workers' compensation claims filed and the actual dollar amount of those claims, by following these four steps:

1. Conduct thorough pre-employment background screening to eliminate those individuals likely to end up as claimants (i.e., those with a history of frequent claims).

2. Implement a get-tough drug policy to keep work environments safe and claim-free. A regular drug user is five times more likely than a nonuser to file a workers' compensation claim. Drug users also have higher health insurance claims, more on-the-job related accidents and increased absenteeism.

3. Identify suspicious claims early.

4. Investigate all suspicious claims.

Following these steps can help corporations reduce the instances of fraudulent claims and avoid the very real possibility of increased liability. Some warning signs of possible fraudulent workers' compensation claims include:

---

[16] Georgia State. *Fraud and Non-Compliance*. Atlanta: Georgia Board of Worker's Compensation, 1996. Print.

- A delayed notice of injury and/or improper reporting of the injury.

- Friday afternoon claims that are reported at the beginning of the following week.

- An employee fails to show up for work and reports his injury after being off for several days.

- The employee fails to show up for his first doctor's appointment and does not call to cancel, postpone or reschedule the appointment.

- The employee cannot find the words to express the pain he is experiencing and is overly dramatic.

- There are frequent changes of physicians, or requests to change physicians. There are previous claims of this nature.

The cumulative costs of fraud, employee theft, and other forms of internal loss always far outweigh the relatively small investment that can be made in the area of security and prevention. When every department in a company is being pressured into reducing operating expenses to stay competitive, the drains on company profits because of fraud or theft and the loss of productivity because of drug use or improper workers' compensation claims cannot be overlooked.

Be Prepared for Labor Strikes

Corporations need to assess their risk for potential labor strikes and the possibility of associated violence. Having the correct mixture of a security presence in place could save your company thousands of dollars in damages and perhaps actually save lives.

The "correct mixture of a security presence" means the involvement of the law enforcement community and an on-site uniformed security force. The security force should be a professionally run organization that can provide security for your property during those times when there is an increased likelihood of sabotage. They should be able to both enhance the safety of the employees who are working and protect the product flow for your business. (Note that not all security agencies are equipped to handle most situations involving criminal activity on a scale associated with something akin to a labor strike.) It is the local police agency, however, that will have the lion's share of responsibility in the event of a strike. Therefore it would be an excellent idea to develop a good working relationship with them, as well as the state police or highway patrol.

During your discussions with the police, make sure to address the topic of labor strikes, and work with them on developing pre-strike and post-strike action plans.

A pre-strike action plan will outline exactly what will be done to protect the company's sensitive and important documents, electronic and other technical equipment, as well as products and services. This plan should also include items such as lighting, fencing and the removal of waste or other hazardous materials that could be an environmental concern. The plan should address the issues of emergency equipment, alarm systems, medical supplies, vendor notification, and meetings with the non-striking employees about the procedures to be followed during the strike, including the crossing of picket lines.

A post-strike action plan should outline what procedures will be taken by the police to identify any people involved in criminal activity. Usually undercover officers can handle these assignments and can videotape the activities of the strikers. Uniformed officers must be present in sufficient numbers to thwart criminal activity.

Corporate Security and Terrorism

As we all know now, terrorism is a growing reality in our country and in many countries overseas. We will always remember the date of September 11, 2001, as well as we remember December 7, 1941. I shudder to think about the dates that might be added to those; I'm certain that they will come.

In 1970, approximately 300 terrorist attacks of one sort or another were reported in the United States. Twenty years later, that figure had grown to 4,200. And now it has certainly become more difficult to accurately track those numbers, since they very nearly double upon themselves each year. About a full one-third of all domestic terrorist attacks are aimed directly at businesses and business owners. And our people and interests overseas are being attacked, as well.

According to former Federal Bureau of Investigation director William H. Webster, in Benjamin Netanyahu's book, *Terrorism - How The West Can Win*, "For years Americans as individuals have been a favorite target of terrorists around the world. We are regarded as an enemy by many countries and movements that use terrorism.[17]" Americans who are potential targets for terrorism include corporate executives, those who travel overseas, and who make personal decisions for a company or American workers.

Mr. Robert Quigley, the former head of the FBI Bomb Data Center, stated in a recent address to the National Press Club that 40 to 50 percent of the attacks against American-owned businesses and their staffs are perpetrated through the use of bombs or other incendiary devices; a full 60 percent of all terrorist attacks use bombs. He also stated that only about 2 percent of the bomb attacks were preceded by threats. Mr. Quigley went on to say that the focus of the terrorist attacks is to kill people, and that the terrorist agenda is one of hatred and of "getting even." He stated that even though "only" a few hundred to perhaps a few thousand people are killed each year by bombs compared to the 25,000 to 40,000 killed each year in the United States by other means, it is the bombings that grab the headlines and put the terrorist organizations in the spotlight. He believes that companies that do business abroad must have in place bomb-threat management teams[18].

Admiral William Crowe, former chairman of the Joint Chiefs of Staff, stated on July 7, 1999, that any events where large numbers of people gather are attractive to terrorists. That statement has proven true many times since 1999. Admiral Crowe predicted with accuracy that as we entered the new millennium there would be a dramatic rise in crime rates[19]. Neil Livingston, the chief executive officer for Globaloptions, stated that tourists and others (e.g., employees working overseas) should use extreme caution when traveling. He predicts a "spike in violent crime," including all manner of street crimes and looting[20].

---

[17] Netanyahu, Benjamin. *Terrorism – How the West Can Win*. New York: Farrar, Straus and Giroux, 1987. Print.

[18] Robert Quigley. "Eyes in Gaza." Address, National Press Club. Washington, DC, 2008.

[19] Admiral William Crowe (statement), Washington, DC, 1999.

[20] Neil Livingston, Globaloptions (private conversation), Washington, DC, 2006.

On a personal note, because of my work, I had to make several trips to South America from 1984 to 1996, to places that included areas around Bogota and Medellin in Colombia. On one of the last trips I was approached by three people who attempted to assault and rob me. Despite the experience and diligence I thought I had, I was still spotted as an American. On another occasion, during an assignment to the Balkans in 1996, I had my truck punctured by rifle fire while traveling through some mountainous areas. All of this just goes to show that there are places overseas where Americans must be extremely cautious.

Most people in the corporate arenas are at risk, but despite the overall increase in attacks on business executives, some chief executive officers are continuing business and travel as usual, while some others have wisely tightened their security.

In a survey of Fortune 1000 companies' chief executives, more than half said they no longer travel to high-risk destinations in other countries, and one-third said they avoid specific commercial airlines with a history of being targets[21]. Another sector of corporate America, however, maintains a rather relaxed attitude towards international terrorism. Many smaller companies feel that the risk is too small to justify any expense to protect employees and assets, while other companies believe that terrorism is limited only to high-risk or high-profile executives.

We should remember that no matter what the motivation may be, whether it's political, religious or something else, terrorists are criminals. And terrorist acts are criminal acts. Therefore, the steps we take to avoid the terrorists are essentially the same steps that must be taken to avoid the criminals. According to figures quoted by Interpol in a 2001 symposium on the subject, the majority of kidnappings, assassination attempts and other attacks occur when people are leaving or arriving home; a full 80 percent occur in or near the individual's automobile[22].

---

[21] Walker, Donald. *Top Security Threats and Management Issues Facing Corporate America*. Washington, DC: publisher, 2002.

[22] Jacques Sedonate. Interpol Symposium. Lyon, France, 2001.

Chapter Five

Airport and Airline Security

The tragic events of September 11, 2001, and the worldwide events following that date have changed the way we live and work. Many of the changes were made in the airport environments. A recent audit report by the Department of Transportation's (DOT) Office of the Inspector General (OIG), however, shows that the Federal Aviation Administration's (FAA) oversight of access control at airports in the United States is inadequate[23].

During their investigation, OIG agents penetrated secure airport areas by "piggy-backing" (following) employees through doors, riding unguarded elevators, walking through cargo facilities and driving through unmanned gates. OIG agents boarded a number of U.S. and foreign airliners unchallenged, and in some instances were "seated and ready for departure at the time we concluded our tests," the group says.

Not surprisingly, the FAA has restricted access to the OIG's report, saying it "contains some sensitive security information." In its conclusion, the OIG says airline and airport workers often ignore FAA security procedures, and that the FAA has been "slow to strengthen" its security oversight.

Several years ago, I conducted a study for Embry-Riddle Aeronautical University, entitled *Airport and Airline Security - A Matter of Fences and Fixed Attitudes*. During the course of the study I managed to easily breach security at a number of large airports in the United States, including the Daytona Beach International Airport right next to the university. In most cases I was not challenged by anyone during those excursions, and on one occasion at Dulles International Airport outside of Washington, D.C., I was even assisted by an unwitting airport employee, who allowed me to board first a Russian and then a French airliner.

That study was conducted prior to September 2001, but with the exception of the primary passenger control areas in most airports, little has changed. I only mention this to point out just how vulnerable we actually are in America. Not only should we be concerned about the

---

[23] United States. *FAA Audit -2006*. Washington, DC: Department of Transportation, 2006. Print.

destinations to which we travel, but we should also be aware that the FAA has done a less than admirable job in providing any real security at our nation's airports.

Crimes in Terminals

Baggage Theft

One of the most common problems at airports is the theft of baggage, and it is without a doubt one of the toughest crimes to control. In the confusion that is the reality of today's airport environment, it's easy to get caught up in the process of hectically coordinating your arrangements. Being at the right terminal on time to make a connecting flight, quickly using rest-room facilities, getting a quick bite to eat at a restaurant, talking on a mobile phone, finding your checked baggage on a conveyor belt, or trying to rent a car—all can easily be distracting. And it is that moment's distraction that a criminal is looking for. In this environment, passengers will frequently put down briefcases and luggage.

According to Inspector John Boland (Retired) of the Port Authority of New York and New Jersey, "it's amazing to me what people put into a briefcase—maybe $80,000 to $100,000— and then walk away.[24]"

At the Miami International Airport and a few others around the country, announcements are broadcast over the public address systems warning passengers to keep close watch of their property. Information booths at some airports provide security brochures, while other airports apparently don't want to alarm passengers and therefore provide little, if any, information. One of those airports is the Orlando International Airport, which prides itself on tourist attractions, such as Disney World. This is most unfortunate and is a disservice to the traveling public.

So, the bottom line must be for us to be extremely cautious and aware of our surroundings. Never let your property out of your sight for even a moment. If you're leaving on a flight, at some point you will be required to place your carry-on bags—including briefcases, handbags, lap-top computers, camera bags, coats and jackets, and

---

[24] Inspector John Boland (Retired), Port Authority of New York and New Jersey (statement), 2005.

whatever else you might have—on a conveyor belt to be scanned. And then, of course, you must walk through a metal-detector bridge or full-body X-ray scanner. And it's at this point when the crime can occur.

Here's what typically happens: You will be singled by a pair of criminals. (To be effective, criminals normally operate in pairs.) Criminals like to victimize people who appear preoccupied or vulnerable. They can obviously see that sooner or later you will have to place your carry-on items on that conveyor belt. They will often choose a time when the airport is especially busy or congested, and they will often target a harried mother with her children. As you stand in line waiting to place those carry-on items on the conveyor belt, the pair of criminals will stand in line in front of you.

The first criminal effortlessly walks through the metal detector bridge and begins to retrieve his carry-on items. The second criminal, however, (the one right in front of you) will be delayed because he has set off the metal detector, and it will take him several tries to get through the bridge without setting the thing off. In the meantime your carry-on items have long since gone through the scanner tunnel and have come out the other side. While you were patiently waiting for the person in front of you to finally make it through the bridge, and while he has successfully blocked your view (he's always the larger of the two criminals), the first idiot has easily taken your handbag or briefcase and has walked away.

He may not go to the gates, but may at some point walk back out into the terminal area. He will quickly blend in with the throngs of people while you are still frantically looking for your missing items. And, of course, his accomplice, (who was right in front of you) is nowhere to be seen.

The one popular variation to this is where the criminal is behind you, and as you place your carry-on items on the conveyor belt and walk through the metal-detector bridge, he has quickly grabbed one or two of the items before they made it too far into that little tunnel. He then walks away in the opposite direction.

Arguably, the instances of these types of crimes have decreased a small percentage since the increase in airport security that followed the hijacking of those four airplanes on September 11, 2001, but the criminals have not been stopped entirely. Their activities continue to expose holes in airport security that prompt the imposition of increasingly tight security procedures.

One enterprising moron at Chicago's O'Hare International Airport recently obtained a ticket on a United Airlines flight. The flight was scheduled to depart around 4:45 p.m., and his first trip through the metal detector bridge was at 2:02 p.m. By 3:50 p.m., he had walked back through four more times, in the process stealing nine items: two laptop computers, two briefcases, one handbag, one camera bag and three other plastic shopping bags containing recently purchased merchandise. He never did make his flight, though. Following his last excursion, he was arrested entering an automobile driven by an accomplice. Authorities found all the stolen items inside the trunk of the car, along with some other merchandise apparently stolen earlier in the day from a local department store.

Although it's reassuring to see armed National Guard soldiers at some airport security checkpoints, criminals like the one in Chicago are still busy. And don't assume that the uniformed Transportation Security Administration agents who scan the carry-on items will have the slightest idea that any of your articles are missing. The TSA folks are trained to see what's inside of those bags; they don't concentrate on who is taking what off of the other end of the conveyor belt. These people are only minimally trained and are paid very low wages. Even with the federal government taking responsibility for the screeners, not a lot has changed. The criminals know all this, and they also know that you may be so preoccupied that you may not give a great deal of attention to your belongings. They are also aware that a great many people keep their valuables—such as jewelry, cash and credit cards—in their carry-on bags and not in their checked luggage.

Here are some things you can do to prevent becoming a victim in this environment:

> While you're waiting in line at the airline ticket counter, make sure to keep a close watch on your luggage. Also keep a watchful eye on the person directly behind you. You could be in line for several minutes, and by the time you actually make it to the ticket counter, several valuable items could be missing from your luggage or carry-on bags.

> If you stop for a quick bite to eat at an airport restaurant or a drink at the bar, keep a close eye on your belongings. If you were to hang your handbag or other item over the back of the seat, it would be out of your immediate control and could be easily accessed by a thief.

➤ When you have to place your carry-on items on that conveyor belt, pause for just a moment to allow the person in front of you to clear the metal detector bridge. Then place your bag on the belt, making sure that the bag actually goes into the tunnel to be scanned and not into the hands of the guy behind you.

➤ While watching carefully for your bags to come out the other end, walk right through the metal detector bridge to retrieve your belongings. As long as you have not set off the metal detector, you should be able to walk right through quite quickly. If the metal detector does go off, make sure to keep your eyes on your property. The screeners will understand your concerns about this.

➤ Once you make it through the metal detector bridge or full-body X-ray scanner, if you're pulled aside for a closer inspection, as typically happens today, you will be separated from your carry-on items as well as perhaps your watch and rings, etc., that were all placed in the little basket. Don't lose sight of those items. This is a perfect opportunity for a thief to strike.

Pickpockets

Other problems that travelers could face at the airport are pickpockets and purse snatchers. When it comes to your handbag or wallet, be sure to follow this advice:

➤ If you are carrying a purse, make sure that the strap is over your head or shoulder, and carry the purse under your arm and against your body.

➤ If your purse has a flap for an opening, try to keep the flap side against your body. You could even carry the purse under your coat.

➤ If you carry a wallet in your back pocket, make sure that the button on the pocket is secure.

> Consider putting your credit cards in a pocket and not in the wallet. Also consider leaving your cash (bills) folded in a pocket.

Many foreign tourists prefer to keep their money in briefcases rather than wallets. Thieves know this and will target the briefcases, but the wallet remains a prize because that's where the credit cards are. The handbag usually holds both cash and the credit cards. My advice, again, is to carry cash in a front pocket and credit cards in another pocket. If at all possible, use travelers' checks and leave everything else at home.

Remember that, at the airport, there could be hundreds of people around you, and there is likely to be a certain amount of contact with others. Be extremely wary of someone who "accidentally" bumps into you. You may soon realize that your wallet is missing.

While conducting a study for airport security, Mike Gleason, a security consultant, once told me, "There are hundreds of scams multiplied by thousands of people perpetrating them.[25]" One of the favorite scams used against people at airports and elsewhere is where a criminal "accidentally" spills a substance such as ketchup on a traveler. The criminal apologizes, while wiping the substance off of the victim. At the same time a second criminal is busy stealing the victim's briefcase or luggage, or whatever he can quickly take. You must be on guard for any uninvited contact. If something like this happens, immediately move away from the people and don't allow them to get near you. If you are suspicious of someone, try to get help right away. Most airport police are trained to deal with these types of situations.

Crime in the Air

While on board U.S. domestic carriers, passengers are subject to federal laws. Any violations of law on those flights, which would otherwise be handled by state or local authorities, would be prosecuted by federal authorities. Advise a flight crew member if you believe a violation of the law has or is being committed on board a flight.

Documented cases of on-board opportunistic theft are on the rise. According to Richard Allen, a former airline security analyst,

---

[25] Mike Gleason, airport security consultant (statement), 2010.

"There once existed a preconceived notion that crime just didn't occur inside the airplane. That idea has long since gone by the boards." In an interview conducted in his home in the United Kingdom, Mr. Allen stated, "All forms of on-board crime, while not taken for granted, are now more or less expected from time to time.[26]"

If, while on-board a flight, you have to leave your seat for any reason, make sure you know where your money, credit cards and any other valuables are. If they're under your seat in a carry-on bag or even in the overhead bin, trying to convince yourself that the nice gentleman sitting next to you on the flight is as honest as the day is long may not be a good idea.

Just as an aside, while we're on the subject of airports and airplanes, I have to mention what seems to be a relatively new trend in criminal activity. To show just how nuts things are really getting, it seems that the criminals have gotten the idea that helicopters can help them commit crimes. (They must have all seen that Charles Bronson movie.) In Port Moresby, New Guinea, five men were shot dead in a gun battle with police after hijacking a helicopter as part of a bank robbery attempt. Dressed in military uniforms, the heavily armed crooks landed on the roof of the PNG Banking Corporation Building and made their way into the public area. Tipped off in time, police swarmed the area and opened fire on the thieves, forcing the would-be robbers to retreat to their helicopter and attempt a takeoff. Police in the street fired on the rotorcraft, damaging it enough to force a crash landing in the street, where the five criminals were killed. Amazingly the hijacked pilot managed to escape the wreckage unharmed.

In another hijacking attempt that evidently went wrong, Brazilian pilot Jose Claudio Valerio was found dead, apparently killed by a passenger in flight. The helicopter came down near the town of Maris de Fe in the southern Brazilian state of Minas Gerais. Because the cause of Valerio's death was a gunshot wound to the neck, police theorized that he was killed by one of the two men who hijacked the helicopter. After the helicopter crashed, the two hijackers emerged from the wreckage with only slight injuries and disappeared after they were taken to a local hospital.

In the north of Italy, two men recently stole a helicopter from a small airport and flew it to the only bank in town. Neither men were pilots and managed to crash the helicopter into the side of the bank.

---

[26] Richard Allen, (statement), Liverpool, United Kingdom. 2001.

Both of the men were killed in the crash, and both had lengthy criminal records.

Just in case you think this stupidity only happens somewhere else, two women hijacked a helicopter at gunpoint in Keystone Heights, Florida, and ordered the pilot to fly to the nearby Union Correctional Institution to stage a breakout. (That prison facility is home to many of Florida's death row inmates.) Upon arrival, however, the hijackers apparently lost their nerve and abandoned the attempt as the rotorcraft approached the jail. They then told the pilot to return to Keystone Heights Municipal Airport, where they fled in a car. They were subsequently arrested and charged with armed kidnapping.

Chapter Six

How to Stay Safe as a Tourist in the United States

In recent years, the numbers of crimes committed against foreign tourists in the United States has increased dramatically. American tourists visiting vacation destinations are also targeted. Fueling the increase is the seeming inability to incarcerate and keep violent career criminals in prison.

One does not have to go beyond the daily newspaper or the television newscast to hear the awful details of murders, rapes and armed robberies perpetrated against innocent tourists. In Florida, one of the places where I was a law enforcement officer for a number of years, it was not unusual to hear about a German tourist being fatally shot while en route to his hotel, or a gentleman from Great Britain being murdered while asleep at a rest stop. It became so hazardous to drive on the highways of Florida that the governor decided to have security guards stationed at rest stops and to appoint a new Highway Patrol director, all in a failed effort to curb the violence. The Highway Patrol director soon left his post and, supposedly because of the lack of funding, the guards were taken away from the rest stops. Many of the rest stops, by the way, have since been closed in an apparent effort to save money for the state. But the reality is that the rest stops that do remain open in Florida and in many other locations are dangerous places.

During that same time, the state of Florida continually resisted the need to build more prisons to house the overwhelming volume of violent offenders. And because of the ill thought-out programs initiated by former Attorney General Janet Reno when she worked in Dade County prior to her years with the Clinton administration, much of the funding that should have been earmarked for the construction of much-needed prisons went instead to typical liberal "feel good" programs designed to rehabilitate and educate extremely violent career criminals. All of those programs failed miserably, and what makes this situation so incredibly awful is that because of the lack of prison facilities, those same violent offenders were set free to commit more crimes. Lest someone have the impression that I have something against the state of Florida, let me just say that a great many states find themselves in more or less the same set of circumstances.

John Douglas, an author and former special agent with the Federal Bureau of Investigation, has stated that it is impossible to rehabilitate certain violent criminals[27]. He has been called to investigate many high-profile cases, such as the O.J. Simpson and JonBenét Ramsey cases and others, and continues to represent the victims of violence. His views on the subject are certainly worth merit, and his opinions regarding the issues of violent criminals need to be remembered. As a society we must learn how to cope in an ever-increasing world of violence.

If I were a tourist coming to the United States, I would be extremely cautious if I traveled to New York, California or Florida, and I would prepare myself for the very real possibility that I could be a victim. This is actually a possibility in just about all fifty states, but because of the attractions and the weather, as well as the criminal element, the risk is particularly high in states like Florida.

If the liberal governors don't have the backbone to enact strong laws to keep the violent career criminals in prison, and they don't have the political will to build the facilities needed to house the criminals, what can be done to keep citizens and tourists safe in our country?

Precautions You Can Take

Planning Your Trip

If you believe you could be targeted during your trip because of a political persuasion, religious affiliation, governmental or judicial position, or any of a number of other reasons, choose your airline carefully, and fly nonstop whenever possible. (El Al Airlines, by the way, has a record of security that is difficult to match[28,29]) If you are in this high-risk category, you may want to have a security agent travel ahead of you by a day or so to have everything ready for your arrival. Or you can hire a security firm in the United States who will prepare everything ahead of time. If you do not have a security agent, arrange to travel with a companion.

---

[27] John Douglas, Former FBI Agent (statement), 2004.

[28] Melton, Keith H. U.S. *Guide to Surviving Terrorism*. New York: Harper Publishing, 2009. Print.

[29] Anonymous security representative of Mossad, (statement), 2010.

Before departing your home to come to the United States (and this is applicable for Americans traveling within the country), learn as much as you can about your destination. Call, write, or go on-line to the local Chamber of Commerce and request their information packets. Once you have this information, study the maps closely. At the very least, be familiar with the highway systems that take you from the airport to your hotel, and from the hotel to the places you intend to visit. You could get on the Internet and obtain most of the information you'll need.

While on your flight, go over your plans and maps with your family. Be focused, rested and mentally aware. Remember that you're heading for an airport environment, a place rife with opportunities for you to become a victim, as we discussed in the last chapter.

After You Arrive

Here are some other precautions to take once you arrive in the U.S.:

> If possible, have a friend pick you up at the airport. This will eliminate a great deal of anxiety and aggravation.

> Take precautions when renting a car. Make sure that the car you are renting does not have a car-rental bumper sticker on it, or license plates indicating that the car is a rental. (In Florida for example, license plates for rental cars used to begin with the letters Y or Z.) Many criminals know what to look for in order to victimize you, and these things could be a clear sign that you are a tourist who is unfamiliar with the area. The rental representative should be helpful with this, but if not, you must demand that your car does not have those types of license plates. The laws have changed regarding this issue, and rental companies have to comply. If you do find that your car has one of those bumper stickers on it, just remove it and throw it away. Removing those bumper stickers from rental cars does not violate any statute that I know of.

> Before leaving the rental area, make sure that you understand all of the vehicle's controls. Looking for those

controls while you're actually driving in traffic is a distraction and obviously dangerous.

> Also, make sure that your luggage and packages are secured out of sight in the trunk of your car. If the car doesn't have a trunk, at least put the things out of sight as much as possible. (And never leave valuables in your car unattended.)

> Make sure that all the doors of your car are locked and that all of the windows are up. (Using seat belts and child-restraint devices are required. If you did not bring a child restraint device with you, the rental agencies have them.)

> While en-route to your destination, be alert and aware of where you are. If you become lost, do not pull over to the side of the road to study your map or directions right away. A much better idea is to find a well-lit and public place for this. Make sure that you keep the doors locked and the windows up.

> Absolutely do not pick up hitchhikers under any circumstances. Many of the hitchhikers along our highway systems today have extensive criminal histories. If you are lost and decide to ask directions from someone, stop at a service station or a garage. Better yet, stop at a fire or police station. Remember that the police are there to serve you, and the vast majority of them are highly trained, motivated and caring individuals who will assist you in any way they can.

> In all circumstances, make sure that you park in well-lit areas. Before you enter your car, make sure that you check the inside and underneath, as well as the immediate surrounding area, for anyone who may be hidden from view.

> If you are stopped in traffic, always leave enough room between you and the car in front of you so that you can drive around it if necessary. Never let your car idle in neutral. You may well need to accelerate away quickly in

the event that someone approaches you. (And if you have a flat tire and are approached by someone who may be suspicious, you can still accelerate away quickly on the rim of the wheel.)

> In the event that you are approached by someone who demands your money or valuables, it is probably better not to resist. Your safety and well-being, and that of your family, should be your foremost concern. If violence is imminent, however, you must resist like a demon possessed. Your life could depend on this.

> Don't exit a highway in order to avoid a toll. The tolls may be an inconvenience, but it's much better to just pay the toll than to become lost.

> If you're having car trouble, pull over to the side of the roadway as far as possible and park. Use the emergency or four-way flashers. Keep the doors locked and the windows rolled up while you await the arrival of a law enforcement officer. On most highways in America, you won't have to wait too long for the police to arrive. If someone other than a police officer stops to assist you, keep the windows rolled up and shout for them to leave. Do not allow them access to you or your vehicle. You could shout for them to call the police. I have also heard the advice that if you have mechanical problems with your car you should indeed pull off the roadway as far as possible, park and use the emergency flashers, but then exit your vehicle and stand away from it as you await the arrival of the police. By doing this, you would be far enough away from your car that if it were struck from behind by another vehicle, you would be out of harm's way.

Be aware that several ploys have been used by criminals to distract drivers or to get them to stop. If, as an example, you are bumped from behind, do not pull over and stop. Instead, drive to the nearest well-lit public area and dial 911 to call police for assistance. The police should know exactly where you are as soon as you call and should arrive in short order. You can use any public telephone in America to dial 911, and you do not have to deposit any coins to do so.

If you have a cell phone, you can also dial 911, but you may have to give the police your location. If you're driving along a highway and you call 911, just give the police the name of the highway (e.g., "Route 95") and the mile marker you are passing. (The mile markers are on the side of the highways on slender vertical, white metal posts.) You will have to tell police the direction in which you are heading (north, south, east or west) as well as a description of your vehicle (or the description and license plate of a suspect vehicle). Within a very short time, you will have police vehicles all around you. Keeping in mind the criminals' goal to distract you:

> If you are told by a passing motorist, or anyone, that something is wrong with your car, do not stop; contact the police. If someone indicates that they are in need of assistance, do not stop. Again, go somewhere safe to call the police or use your cell phone.

> Likewise, if a car approaches you from behind and flashes its headlights at you to make you pull over, or uses a small dash- or roof-mounted emergency light (usually blue or red in color) to signal you to stop, do not stop. Instead, go to a well-lit area and call the police right away. If the vehicle follows you, do not stop. These types of signals are not normally used by the police in the United States. Some police vehicles have those dash-mounted lights, but they are usually used in concert with extremely bright strobe lights mounted internally behind the car's grille. When they are used, even the headlights flash, and you can be somewhat confident that the driver is a police officer. If, on the other hand, an undercover police officer uses one of the small dash- or roof-mounted lights and you don't stop, he or she will know that you are suspicious and concerned and will call a regular patrol car to pull you over, if needed. Anyone, including criminals, can purchase the dash- and roof-mounted lights, so just make sure that the person pulling you over is a law enforcement officer.

At Your Hotel

If you've made it safely to your hotel, motel, resort complex or bed-and-breakfast, congratulations. But, now is not the time to let your guard down. According to Anthony G. Marshall, an attorney and Dean of the School of Hospitality Management at the Florida International University in Miami, "More than ever, security is the hotel guest's number-one priority.[30]" He advises that "safety first," at your home-away-from-home should be paramount in your thinking. Here are some things to keep in mind when securing lodging:

> *Find out about your room:* Prior to your trip, find out if the room can be entered from the building's exterior. Some motels have doors that open into the parking lot or common walkways. It is much better if ground floor doors lead into an interior lobby or hallway. If you are not entirely comfortable with the ground floor arrangement, insist that you have a room on the second floor or above. On some upper floors, the relationship between location and security may be problematic. Some hotels, as an example, try to place female guests in rooms near an elevator so that they will not have to walk down long hallways to get to their rooms. Others, however, maintain that elevators and stairways afford a quick exit, and that long hallways may actually give women the opportunity to determine if they are being followed. Use your good instincts. Again, if you are not comfortable with the arrangement, insist that the hotel changes your room.

> *Find out about security:* Regarding the actual security arrangements in place for the building, you should ascertain if there are security officers on duty. Most small hotels and motels, as well as bed and breakfast inns, obviously will not have any security guards, but the larger establishments in major urban areas should indeed provide this service.

> *Find out about surveillance systems:* Additionally, a closed circuit television monitoring system should be in place. By the way, a system that is monitored infrequently is useless. It is much preferable to have the systems monitored 24 hours each day by trained security officers.

---

[30] Anthony G. Marshall, Dean of the School of Hospitality Management at the Florida International University in Miami, (statement), 2004.

➤ *Find out about parking-lot security:* Security should be maintained in the parking lot as well. A limited number of entrances and exits, and high fences should be the norm. The parking lot should be very well lit using high intensity lighting, and the lot itself should have a uniformed presence at all times.

➤ *Find out about crime in the area:* Ask the hotel management if there have been instances of criminal activity. They have a legal obligation to answer those questions truthfully. Feel free to contact the local area law enforcement agency to see what crimes have been committed on or about the hotel property. They will certainly let you know. By law, they must let you know.

When making your room reservation, try to avoid hotel rooms that share balconies. Get as much information as you can about your room:

➤ If your room has a balcony or exterior access with a sliding glass door, make sure there are effective locks with a secondary security lock in place.

➤ Your hotel room door should be equipped with a peephole or view port. Most hotel rooms have these installed, but it doesn't hurt to check. Some will have a window with a good view of the area outside of the door. Use all of these to your advantage. Some historic properties or bed-and-breakfast inns may not have any of these features.

➤ Ask if the doors to your hotel room lock automatically when the door is closed. If not, at the very least. they should be equipped with locks that allow you to lock up when leaving.

➤ The lock should have at least a one-inch deadbolt that cannot be opened with a master key or room key when the guest has locked it from the inside. If there is an adjoining room next to your hotel room, the connecting door should have a deadbolt lock, as well.

➤ Ask if your hotel has electronic card keys. These are by far the best, as they can be easily replaced or the combination can be changed frequently. The combinations should be changed after each guest has checked out. Contact the hotel to find out if this is their policy.

➤ If the hotel uses keys rather than the electronic cards, the keys should be blank, without any room numbers or other identification on them. If the hotel still uses the keys with the plastic or metal "Drop in any mailbox" tags that contain the name and the address of the hotel — and very often the actual room number — go to another hotel. While we're on this subject, some hotels use the cross-coding method, wherein the number on the key is actually different than the room number. Some of these are much too simplistic. Often a single digit is added or subtracted from the front or back of the actual room number. Thieves aren't that stupid, and will easily figure this out.

Once you've reached your hotel, follow these precautions:

➤ Do not display your room key in public or leave it about carelessly. It can be easily stolen. The hotel restaurant or bar, or perhaps the swimming pool, are all places where keys and other valuables can be stolen.

➤ Make sure the hotel staff should have extremely limited access to your room, and that the access times are recorded by the hotel. Make certain that the hotel understands your concerns regarding this issue, and that there is a stringent policy in place regarding who is allowed into the room. Also, understand that if you do not want a maid or anyone else in your room, the hotel has an obligation to follow your wishes. The maid can be instructed to leave clean towels, sheets, other linens and bathroom necessities in a bag outside of your door.

➤ Contact the hotel staff to find out their opinion about the safe places to travel in the area, as well as the places to avoid. If there is an issue of personal security with your visit relating to the threat of terrorism, you might consider making hotel reservations in someone else's name.

> While at your hotel, maintain a low profile and choose comfortable and casual attire; avoid excessive alcohol intake.

> Do not draw attention to yourself by displaying any amounts of cash or jewelry. It's a much better idea to leave the expensive jewelry back at home in your safety deposit box while you're away on vacation or holiday. Thieves love necklaces and Rolex watches. Use the hotel safe if you have brought along some of these items.

> Be ever suspicious of strangers who are too forward. Keep the purpose of your visit confidential and never leave company documents or personal papers anywhere (especially your hotel room) unattended.

> Absolutely do not allow any stranger into your room, under any circumstances. You don't even have to answer the door, but, as I suggested in chapter two, it may be a better idea to ask who is at the door without actually opening it. If the person at the door claims to be a hotel employee, call the lobby right away and ask why someone from the staff is trying to access your room.

> Likewise, do not invite strangers into your room. Gentlemen, we know you may be away from home on that business trip or convention, and that beautiful woman you met is so very distracting, but circumstances can quickly change. I have lost count of the number of times big, burly men have been reduced to tears because they have been robbed by prostitutes or transvestites. Don't think that it can't happen to you.

> If you're returning to the hotel late at night, use the main lobby entrance, and look around before entering the parking lot.

> Whenever you enter your hotel room, close the door securely behind you right away and use all of the locking mechanisms on the door. You should at this time check the connecting room doors, windows and sliding glass doors to ensure that they are all secure.

> Do not leave your luggage unattended in your room, and as an extra precaution, use either your business address or a trusted friend's address on your luggage identification tags.

While staying at the hotel, report any suspicious activity to hotel management. If they do not satisfactorily respond to your concerns, call the police, and then file a complaint with the hotel.

Attitude Is Everything

In the United States, I have often heard it said that attitude is everything, and in many ways this is true. If you have the right attitude, if you have a confident air about you, and if you carry yourself properly, people will leave you alone. I am only 5 feet 10 inches tall, and I weigh about 160 pounds. This is small for a police officer, but I always have a look on my face at the right moment that says "you better not get in my way." It's worked for me for the last 44 years or so, and it can work for you.

I do recall one wonderful exception to this rule. About seven years ago, a gentleman from Wales and his family were visiting the Orlando, Florida, area. They were staying at a hotel on the Orange Blossom Trail in Orlando, an area that has become a hotbed of criminal activity. One evening, when the family was getting out of their rented car in the hotel parking lot, they were approached by three men who demanded all of their money and jewelry. The three would-be thieves had picked the wrong man to victimize. As it turned out, the gentleman from Wales was a professional boxer with all sorts of European titles to his credit. All three idiots ended up in an area hospital (two with a variety of broken bones and facial injuries, and the third with a concussion). Soon after the incident, I interviewed my hero from Wales, and with one look at the man you could easily tell that this gentleman was someone who was not to be trifled with. He had the look of a warrior. His facial features appeared to be chiseled from granite and his arms were as big as my thighs. So why would the three morons pick on this family? I honestly don't know the answer to that. They may have just been a little extra stupid, or perhaps the parking lot lighting was not that good. But whatever the reason, the three went to prison just as soon as they were released from the hospital.

Usually, however, if you have the right attitude and look, and if you're prepared, aware, suspicious and alert, you will be fine. Enjoy your vacation.

Chapter Seven

The World's Most Dangerous Destinations

The fifth of July, 1841, was an auspicious day for the world of travel. It was the day that 570 passengers traveled by Midland rail to Leicester and back for one shilling. It was the day that Thomas Cook put together the first organized tour. The passengers were members of the local temperance association in Market Harborough, and were on their way to attend a gathering in Loughborough.

But, 150 years later, fifty-eight tourists were shot and stabbed to death in Luxor, Egypt. A busload of children were robbed and raped in Guatemala. Three young female tourists were brutally murdered in Yosemite National Park. Eight Greeks were killed because they looked like Israelis. Nine Germans were murdered outside an Egyptian museum in Cairo, Egypt. In Uganda in 1998, eight gorilla trekkers were slaughtered with machetes. Somalis were hijacking and murdering passing yachtsmen. A Yemeni kidnapping turned ugly as 16 people were grabbed and four people were gunned down in a rescue attempt. When four tourists were snatched in southern Iran on August 15, 1999, the kidnappers demanded from the front desk of the hotel, "We need foreigners! How many do you have?"

This is but a very small sampling; the situation throughout many parts of the world has turned chaotic. These are no longer just isolated instances of violence directed against tourists and others. The violence has now become the subject of daily briefings in police squad rooms all over the world. And in many parts of the world there exists near anarchy. Lawlessness has taken hold.

Are you safe traveling overseas? The simple answer is a resounding—no! You could travel to Canada, Scotland, or the southern parts of Ireland, parts of Great Britain and Wales, France, Germany, Iceland, Belgium, Austria, Portugal, Australia, New Zealand and Japan, and remain relatively safe—the key word being "relatively." But, go any farther afield and all bets are off. Even in romantic Italy there is so much street crime—including robberies, thefts and scams directed against tourists—that the police have a hard time keeping up. If you're approached by anyone on the streets of Italy, you'd better be prepared to lose some of your property. And if you carry one of those fanny packs, at some point in your day you will be robbed.

Travel to any of the countries in Central and South America, Africa, the Middle and Far East, Eastern Europe and Russia — literally any of them — and you're fair game.

The Ten Most Dangerous Places

According to Jane Hogan, in a study for the publication *Aviation International News,* civil unrest, political strife and poor economic conditions have resulted in high crime rates in many of the world's cities, prompting widespread safety concerns for foreign travelers[31].

Air Security International, a Houston-based group that ensures the safety of business travelers and corporate air crews, recently released its list of the ten most dangerous locations for foreigners. Included on that list were Algeria, Central Africa, Colombia, Islamabad and Karachi in Pakistan, Johannesburg and Cape Town in South Africa, Lagos and Port Harcourt in Nigeria, Maputo in Mozambique, Mexico City, Port Moresby in Papua New Guinea, and Sao Paulo and Rio de Janeiro in Brazil[32].

Algeria's high level of criminal activity is the result of political and social unrest. There is a high potential for bombings by insurgent groups, as well as abductions and murders, especially for travelers outside city limits.

Similar problems face foreigners in Central Africa, which is besieged by civil wars. Uncontrolled militias rule the streets and often kill on sight. A depressed regional economy has resulted in the country's all-time highest crime rate.

A civil war has raged in Colombia for the last 44 years, resulting in persistent armed conflicts among left-wing guerrillas and right-wing paramilitaries, and the Colombian military forces. American citizens especially have to be cautious here because of the recent enforcement of extradition laws that propose to send drug traffickers and guerrillas to trial in U.S. courts.

Sectarian violence, drive-by shootings, carjackings, residential invasions and drug trafficking are rampant in Pakistan. Groups

---

[31] Hogan, Jane. "Safety Concerns for the Traveling Public." *Aviation International News*, June, 2008.

[32] Hendrix, Alan and Schlotterbeck, Bianca. *World's Most Dangerous Cities*. Air Security International, April, 2010. Print.

operating in Pakistan who are associated with al-Qaeda and their collection of like-minded crazies pose increasing threats to western travelers. In November 1999, there were twelve rocket attacks on American and United Nations targets in Islamabad. In November 2001, following the terrorist attacks in New York and Washington, there were approximately 589 attacks. As I write this book, it has become difficult to properly assess the actual numbers, as they are off the charts and growing by the day.

The South African towns of Johannesburg and Cape Town have been marred by crime. Foreigners in these towns continue to be the targets of carjackings, shootings and terrorist bombings.

Violence is also prevalent in Lagos and Port Harcourt, Nigeria. Criminal activities ranging from pickpocketing to armed robbery occur in all parts of the city. Kidnapping is rampant. Port Harcourt continues to suffer from clashes related to land possession, social demands and tribal rivalries.

The Mozambique capitol of Maputo has a poor economy, which has fueled a growing criminal industry.

In some locations, individuals are prevented from walking in public because of the high risk of armed robberies and kidnappings. The high crime rate in Mexico City continues to increase because of high unemployment, poverty, corruption and drug use. The most common crimes are street robberies, kidnappings and carjackings. But now, large drug gangs have taken over whole swaths of the Mexican countryside. Many of the police agencies there are corrupt from the top to the bottom, and they turn a blind eye to the enormous problem of violent criminal activity.

Port Moresby in Papua New Guinea, has seen an increase in violent crimes, including armed robberies, carjackings, rapes and other sexual assaults. Outside of the city, criminal gangs often set up roadblocks to assault travelers.

Rampant crime can also be seen in the streets of Sao Paulo and Rio de Janeiro, Brazil. Economic recession and high unemployment have increased criminal activity, with a record number of people turning to illegal drug trafficking. Theft is so common that even the country's president had his car stolen in Rio de Janeiro.

This is just the top-ten list, but many of the countries in Africa are now unsafe for travelers, including Egypt, where attacks against foreigners have increased dramatically over the last few years. In addition, many of the east European and former Soviet Union countries are unsafe, especially for American and British tourists.

Travel in the Near and Middle East is also dangerous. Instances of criminal activity directed against foreigners in Lebanon, Syria, Iran and Iraq (and to a lesser extent Jordan) have increased alarmingly. And let's not let Colombia and Brazil stand alone as the places to avoid in South America. Peru, Venezuela and Ecuador are all seeing crime rates increase dramatically.

Strategies to Stay Safe

First, before you start out on your travel abroad, it's a good idea to make copies of your passport and keep one in a safety deposit box; take a second one with you. Copy your travel visa, as well. If your passport ever goes missing, it makes it so much easier to replace. Then, after you arrive at your destination, be sure to check in at the U.S. Embassy before doing anything else.

The following are good bits of advice offered by *The World's Most Dangerous Places* handbook regarding travel into foreign places by tourists and business professionals[33]. They were rewritten for inclusion here.

How to survive on a minibus:

> ➤ Don't travel at night. Many bus lines travel at night because it's cooler and the roads are less crowded, but drunks, rebels, livestock and hidden washouts all seem to be more prevalent at night. Local drivers also like to sleep at night, many of them behind the wheel.

> ➤ Avoid mountainous areas and winter conditions.

> ➤ Bring water and food with you; plan for delays, diversion, and the unexpected.

> ➤ Ask whether the route goes through areas frequented by bandits or terrorist groups. You may be surprised to find out who controls the countryside between major cities.

---

[33] Pelton, Robert Young. *The World's Most Dangerous Places*. New York: Harper Collins, 2010. Print.

> Sit near an exit or on top; make sure you are near a window that opens.

> Remember that your rooftop luggage is prey for rummagers, slashers and thieves. Put your luggage in a standard trash bag, a canvass duffle or under everyone else's.

> Shirt-slashers wait for you to doze off and slip out your money pouches. Put your money in your shoes or boots if you have to.

How to survive taxis:

> Choose your cab rather than let it choose you. Inspect the car first. Hire the oldest taxi driver or the one with the least damage to his car.

> Ask staff at the airport how much the ride should cost to go to the city. Inquire about other methods of transportation.

> Always agree on a total fare first and write the price down and show it to the driver. Ask about luggage, airport or time-of-day surcharges.

> Keep your luggage in the back seat with you — not in the trunk.

> Memorize the local words for "no," "yes," "stop here" and "how much?"

> Have the hotel doorman or guide negotiate cab fares in advance when you plan to tour the city. Many private cars also function as taxis, so don't be surprised if a kind person who picks you up wants money.

> Cab drivers never carry change. Change money at the airport or hotel first.

- Many cabbies will rent themselves out for a flat fee. Do not be afraid to negotiate the services of a trusted cabby as guide, chauffeur and protector of luggage.

- Try to establish a rapport with your driver; he may end up being your best tour guide.

How to survive automobiles:

- Be familiar with local road warning signs and laws. You can be a good driver and be completely baffled by the sign in Urdu that says "washed out bridge ahead."

- Avoid driving yourself, if possible. A local driver may add a few gray hairs, but will be conversant with local laws, shortcuts and safety matters.

- Avoid driving in inclement weather conditions, at nighttime or especially on weekends. You would be surprised what sleeps on the road at night in the tropics. Most locals never venture outside after dark, let alone drive. Fog, rain, drunk drivers and other tourists, kill. In many Central Asian and former Soviet republics, drinking and driving is common. It is estimated that after midnight on every Friday and Saturday night three out of five drivers on the road have been drinking. If you are one of the sober ones, pray that the guy coming from the opposite direction is the second sober driver.

- Stay off the road entirely in high-risk countries. You may think the Italians, Portuguese and Spaniards display amazing bravado as they skid around winding mountain roads, but the accident rate says that they are just lousy drivers who haven't been killed yet.

- Reduce your speed. This is your single biggest edge in staying alive.

- Wear a seat belt, rent bigger cars, drive during daylight, use freeways, and carry a map and a good road guide.

➤ Don't drive tired or while suffering from jet lag. Don't pull off to the side of the road to nap.

➤ Don't leave possessions in plain sight and try to park in well-lit areas.

How to survive boats:

➤ Wear or have quick access to a life preserver. Don't assume that the large chest labeled "Life Preservers" actually has usable life preservers in it. You are better off in a lifeboat, anyway, because of the cold water and the sharks.

➤ Do not take overcrowded boats. Charter your own or ask when the boat will be less crowded. Overcrowding and rough seas are some of the major reasons for the sinking of small- and medium-sized ships.

➤ Avoid travel in rough weather, or during monsoon or hurricane season.

➤ Stay off the water in areas frequented by pirates. In places such as the southern Philippines, Borneo and Thailand, this includes even pleasure excursions. Those modern-day pirates not only steal everything they can, they will rape and murder. The Indian Ocean along the entire east coast of Africa is prowled by pirates, some of whom venture out 200 to 300 miles.

➤ In cold weather, remember where the covered life rafts are and if there are exposure suits available. Understand the effects and prevention of hypothermia.

➤ On large ships, pay attention to safety and lifeboat briefings and practice going from your cabin to the lifeboat station with your eyes closed (literally).

➤ Keep a small carry-on or backpack with a small amount of extra money, papers and minor survival gear such as water, energy bars, compass and a map. Make it waterproof and a potential life preserver by using one or two garbage bags as a liner.

> Prepare to bring items to prevent seasickness, sunburn, glare, and chapped skin or lips.

How to survive flying:

> Stick to U.S.-based carriers with good safety records, or fly El Al.

> Fly between major airports on nonstop flights.

> Avoid bad weather or flying at night.

> Sit in the back of the plane; the last ten rows usually are left intact during a ground impact. You could sit above the wings and pray that you get thrown clear of the airplane. Sitting at an emergency exit (easier exit in case of a fire or emergency landing) might be just as advisable.

> Avoid small charter aircraft, dirt strips, and non-instrument airfields.

> The smaller the plane, the higher the risk. The poorer the country, the less likely whatever it is that has wings has been properly maintained.

> Avoid national carriers that are not allowed to fly into the United States.

> Avoid military cargo flights, tagging along on combat missions, or flying over active combat or insurgence areas.

> Avoid all older Soviet- or Chinese-made aircraft or helicopters. (I learned this one the hard way.)

> Keep up on what type of aircraft you will be flying on (American and European are preferable), and keep in mind that you usually get what you pay for. Avoid older U.S. and European airplanes that are still being flown by Third

World countries, including the Boeing 707 and 720, the Douglas DC-8 and DC-9, Martin, Convair and Fairchild propeller aircraft, and even the wonderful old DC-3. Also the British Comet, Vanguard, and Vickers Viscount as well as the French Caravelle should be avoided. (They should be in museums or owned by me!)

➢ After all this, remember that travel by airliner is the safest method of transportation, but your odds of surviving a plane crash are about 50 percent, at best.

How to survive trains:

➢ Ask locals whether the train is a target for bandits (this is appropriate in Eastern Europe, Russia, Asia or Africa where terrorists, bandits and insurgents regularly target trains).

➢ Beware of Eastern European train routes where thieves are known to ride as passengers. Sleep with the window cracked open to avoid being gassed (believe it or not).

➢ Stash your valuables in secret spots, making it more difficult for robbers to locate your belongings.

➢ Sit toward the back of the train, which is traditionally the safest area in the event of a collision—unless of course your train is rear-ended. (And you thought Amtrak was bad here in the U.S.!)

➢ If possible, keep your luggage with you at all times. Be nice to the conductor, and he may keep an eye out for you.

➢ Trains are preferable to buses or cars when traveling through mountainous area, deserts and jungles.

Chapter Eight

Crimes Against Women

Part of this chapter is an analysis dealing with the issue of violent crimes committed against women. Most of the statistics for this subject have been provided by the United States Department of Justice. An initial review of the findings may help us to better understand the overwhelming scope of the problem.

According to the Department of Justice, more than 2.5 million women experience violence annually in some fashion or another[34]. That figure is growing, and approaching the 4.7 million mark as this book is being written. Yes, that's right — 4.7 million!

What the Statistics Show

Here are some of the sobering statistics from the studies undertaken by the Department of Justice between 1977 and 1991 and from 1992 up to 2011. The results are somewhat subjective, because many of the victims were understandably reluctant to be completely forthright with the information they gave, as some of the crimes were so horrific in nature. Rape, as an example, is definitely not a crime of passion. It is a crime of violence, domination and control directed against women by their husbands, boyfriends, acquaintances and strangers.

> ➤ Women are about equally likely to experience violence perpetrated by a relative or "intimate" associate as by a mere acquaintance or stranger.

> ➤ Nearly two out of every three female victims of violence were related to, or knew, their attacker.

> ➤ About one in four attacks on females involved the use of a weapon by the offender.

---

[34] United States. *Domestic and Familial Violence.* Washington, DC: Department of Justice. 1977-1991; 1992-2011. Print.

➢ About one in three of the weapons used in these attacks were firearms, as oppose to knives, daggers, blunt objects, vehicles or any of a number of other assorted weapons.

➢ About three out of four female victims of violence resisted the actions of the offender either physically or verbally.

➢ At least one-third of female victims of violence were injured as a result of the crime. (In my view, 100 percent, all, of the victims were injured physically, emotionally or psychologically. And those scars are so hard to erase.)

➢ About half of the women victimized by violence reported the crime to the police; the other half did not.

➢ Among those who did not report the crime, about six in ten said that they considered the matter a private or personal one, or that they felt the offense was minor.

➢ Almost six times as many women victimized by intimates (18 percent to 22 percent), as those victimized by strangers (3 percent to 7 percent), did not report their violent victimization to the police because they feared reprisal by the offender.

➢ Nearly half of the victims of rape perceived the offender to have been under the influence of drugs and/or alcohol at the time of the offense.

➢ It was found that women who were raped by strangers sustained more serious injuries than women who were raped by someone they knew.

➢ Where men were more likely to be victimized by acquaintances or strangers, women were just as likely to be victimized by intimates, such as husbands or boyfriends, as they were to be victimized by acquaintances or strangers.

➤ The rate of violence committed by intimates was ten times greater for females than for males. We've somehow labeled part of this as Domestic Violence.

➤ Rape victimizations involving known offenders were almost twice as likely to occur at or near the victim's home (52 percent) compared to rapes by strangers, which were more likely to occur in an open area or public place (43 percent). However, almost a quarter of all the rapes by strangers reported to the police did occur in or near the victim's home.

➤ Black and Hispanic females had a higher risk of experiencing a crime of violence than white and non-Hispanic females. White females, on the other hand, experienced higher theft victimization than black females.

➤ Hispanic females were more likely to experience a robbery than non-Hispanic females, but Hispanic and non-Hispanic females were equally likely to experience other violent crimes.

➤ Both females and males with higher family incomes experienced fewer crimes of violence than those in the lower income categories. The risk of experiencing a crime of theft was greater for females in the higher income categories than those with lower family incomes. Interestingly however, there was no consistent relationship between rates of theft and family income for males.

➤ Females with either a college degree or some college education had lower theft and victimization rates than females with less education. Women with less education generally experienced higher rates of aggravated and simple assaults than women with more education. For the rates of rape and robbery, however, no significant differences occurred between women in diverse educational categories.

➤ Males who had never been married were the most likely to experience a violent crime, followed by females who were divorced or separated. For crimes of theft, both females and males who had never been married were more likely to be victimized, followed by divorced or separated individuals.

➢ Both females and males residing in central cities experienced the highest rates of both violence and theft, compared to their suburban or rural counterparts. This is changing, however, and it is now found that there is not much difference in the figures. No matter where you live, there is a real potential for violence.

➢ Regarding the demographic characteristics of female victims of rape, robbery and assault, it was found that black females were more than twice as likely to experience a robbery as white females. No significant differences separated females of different races for the rates of rape and of aggravated and simple assault.

➢ Women between the ages of twenty and forty-four were the most likely to experience all types of violent crime.

➢ While the risk of becoming a victim of rape or assault decreases after age thirty-four, women over the age of sixty-five were just as likely to become robbery victims as those between the ages of thirty-five and sixty-four.

➢ Regarding the characteristics of offenders who committed violent crimes against women, it was discovered that, generally speaking, most females were attacked by lone offenders. Robbery was the violent crime most likely to involve more than one offender. Rape was the violent victimization least likely to involve more than one offender; less than 10 percent of all rape victimizations involved more than one offender.

Because multiple-offender victimizations represent very different experiences for female victims, for our purpose, the analysis that follows focuses exclusively on one-on-one incidents of violence.

➢ Female victims of all types of violent crimes were more likely to be victimized by male offenders than female offenders. Females, however, committed about a quarter of all the assaults against other females. That figure remains true today, but slowly that figure is decreasing, and the figures are increasing for the male offenders.

➢ Most violent offenders who victimized females were perceived by the victim to be over 21 years of age.

➢ As previously stated, female victims of rape and aggravated assault were significantly more likely to perceive their attackers to be under the influence of drugs or alcohol than females who experienced a robbery or a simple assault. When the offenders were perceived by female victims to be under the influence of drugs or alcohol, a higher percentage of rape and assault offenders were reported to have been using alcohol rather than other drugs. This is also changing, and it is now commonly believed that alcohol and drugs play an equal role in these violent crimes. For robbers perceived to be under the influence, a higher percentage of them were reported to have been under the influence of drugs rather than alcohol.

➢ In general, violent crime against women was primarily intra-racial. Eight out of ten violent crimes against white women were perpetrated by white offenders. Similarly, almost nine out of ten violent victimizations sustained by black women were committed by black offenders.

➢ Robberies of white females were the victimizations most often interracial. A white female robbery victim was as likely to have been victimized by a black offender as a white offender. Robberies experienced by black females were primarily intra-racial according to the Justice Department.

➢ Regarding the growing problem of family violence (domestic abuse), it has been found that it is somewhat difficult to measure because it most often occurs in relative privacy and the victims are sometimes reluctant to report it because of perceived shame or the fear of reprisals by the offender. Also, many victims are reluctant to report these crimes because they will say that they love their husbands or boyfriends (normally the offenders), or for the sake of the children do not want to break up the family unit.

> Females experience more than ten times as many incidents of violence in a year as males. Remember this point: women face at least ten times the amount of violent crimes as do men.

> Women were just as likely to experience a violent victimization by an intimate or relative (33 percent) as they were to be victimized by an acquaintance (35 percent) or a stranger (31 percent). Family-related violence, however, accounted for only 5 percent of all violent victimizations against men. Men were far more likely to be victimized by an acquaintance (50 percent of all male victimizations) or a stranger (44 percent of all male victimizations) than by an intimate or family member.

Domestic Abuse

Domestic abuse directed against women is a growing problem that cuts across all racial, social, geographical, educational and economic levels of society. It makes absolutely no difference whatsoever what social standing you may have; domestic abuse has reached epidemic proportions. Women in both the U.S. and abroad constantly suffer at the hands of violent male offenders. It's happening in every country, in every city and town, across the globe.

I was recently told about a young Palestinian couple who were having an argument that quickly erupted into violence. The enraged husband tied his young pregnant wife's ankles together and hung her upside down from the living room ceiling. He then took a butcher's knife and cut her ears and nose off of her face. Not finished with his grisly task, he gouged both her eyes out with his fingers, and walked out the door. The woman was discovered by her neighbor and survived the ordeal. She is completely blind, and as I write this is scheduled for reconstructive surgery following the birth of her baby. The man was jailed, but was released the same day, without having to post bond. It's highly unlikely that he'll ever spend time in prison for his crimes, as the Palestinian courts seldom jail men for crimes against women.

In Lisbon, Portugal, a man came home from work and found that his wife did not yet have his dinner ready and waiting on the table. He immediately took his belt off and began beating her with the buckle end of the belt. She fell backwards, striking her head on the kitchen stove, and was killed. He was released from jail the next day, due to "family hardships," and was scheduled for trial for six weeks later.

In Portugal, and in so many others countries, crimes against women simply don't matter. In Communist China, there are literally thousands of undocumented cases each year regarding the brutal treatment of women at the hands of violent and out-of-control men. Those cases remain undocumented because the government in mainland China refuses any and all access to the reports.

In Iran, and in Iraq and Afghanistan prior to the United States and Allied military intervention, there are hundreds of reports each year, some documented, others hidden, of women being accused of unproven cases of adultery (usually by their jealous and ignorant husbands). Those women are either stoned to death by chosen family members and friends, beaten with a whip while tied to a post during a public gathering, or shot in the head. Many women have their faces disfigured by either acid or by a flaming torch put to their heads. The men scream bloody murder if somehow a Koran gets burned, but then turn a blind eye when one of their women receives the same treatment! What is going on?

As I write this, the wife of a prominent businessman in Riyadh, Saudi Arabia, was found drinking tea and eating biscuits in a small restaurant with a gathering of her friends from the university where they took classes together. The gathering of friends included two male classmates. The husband apparently showed little emotion at the restaurant when he walked in, but that evening when he returned home, he flew into a jealous rage and stabbed his young wife to death. She was stabbed 44 times. He was never charged with a crime.

In Russia and China, there are thousands of reported domestic abuse and rape cases each year. Most of the cases go unreported to the police. The female murder rate in Russia has gone up more than 600 percent in the last nine years; an astounding and horrible figure.

Outside of Kabul, Afghanistan, as is the tradition in that country, a twelve-year-old girl married a twenty-one-year-old man, who was a member of the Taliban. On their wedding night, the girl apparently didn't perform sexually as the man had wanted, and he beat her until she was unconscious. The beatings continued for the next seven years, almost on a daily basis. She finally found the courage to run away and hid with friends in the next village. When her husband found where she was, he dragged her away, and took her up into the hills where his Taliban cohorts were located. Once there, several of the "men" held her down, while the husband took a sharp knife and first cut her nose off of her face, and then both ears. He then slashed her long, dark hair off, and left her to die. In the middle of the night, grotesquely disfigured and bleeding, she walked 11 miles to get help. Her husband was never arrested for the horrific crimes. She found help with some American troops and was eventually flown to the United States to undergo a series of surgical procedures designed to restore part of her face.

In San Jose, California, the thirty-two-year-old, unemployed, live-in boyfriend of a nineteen-year-old girl, had a "few beers" and began to slap his girlfriend in the face. The man, who considered himself a karate expert, tied the girl to one of the vertical bedposts in her bedroom with her hands behind her back, then used her for "target practice" (according to the statement given to the police). He kicked her repeatedly in the head and chest. She died on the way to the hospital.

In Albany, New York, a local councilman and civic leader was sitting at his desk at home trying to work on some bills, when his wife of twenty-eight years walked up behind him to see how he was doing. He screamed at her to "get away from me," and with the back of his closed fist struck her in the face. He then dragged her to the basement door, threw her down the stairs, and locked the door behind him. He ended up at a local bar and, upon returning home around 2:30 in the morning, found his wife dead at the foot of the stairs. During the course of the subsequent investigation he waived his right to council and made a full confession to the police.

These are only a few illustrations to prove that violence against women, whether it's rape, assault and battery, robbery, domestic abuse, or any other type of violence does occur everywhere and far more frequently than many studies indicate.

To find an appropriate answer to all of this is far beyond the scope of this text. In a perfect world, we would all have the perfect spouse or partner to spend our entire lives with, and we would all be safe from harm and violence. It's impossible to address all the issues of so very many societies that view women in so many different ways. In our "civilized" society right here in the United States, we have a set of narrowly defined rules (our laws) which we expect all our citizens to follow. Those rules say that it is not appropriate to touch anyone in any manner without the person's express will. But the rules in this country are indeed broken every few seconds, as women are being horrifically raped, brutally beaten and murdered.

How to Protect Yourself

When it comes to the issue of domestic abuse, I offer the following six general guidelines:

1. Safety during a heated or potentially explosive incident.

➢ If an argument seems unavoidable, and we all have them, try to have it in a room or area that has access to an exit, and not in a bathroom or kitchen, or anywhere near weapons.

➢ Practice how to get out of your home safely. Identify which doors, windows, elevators or stairways would be best.

➢ Have a packed bag ready and keep it in an undisclosed, but accessible, place in order to leave quickly.

➢ Identify a neighbor you can talk to about the violence and ask that they call the police if they hear a disturbance coming from your home.

➢ Devise a code word or phrase to use with your children, family, friends and neighbors when you need the police.

➢ Teach your children how to dial 911.

➢ Plan for where you will go if you have to leave home, even if you don't think you will need to.

➢ Use your instincts and judgment.

If you're reading this and telling yourself that all of this applies to you in some way, you need to get away now. For the sake of your children, and for your well-being, you need to get away from the abuser. Do not live in a situation like this and think that he's going to change. He will not ever change. He will only get worse, and one day in the not-too-distant future, he could harm your children, as well.

2. Safety when preparing to leave

➢ Call your local domestic violence agency to find out the necessary steps in your area on how to obtain a restraining order. Normally, they can be easily obtained from the courthouse in your town.

➢ Open a savings account in your own name to start to establish or increase your independence. Use the address of a trusted friend or a post office box. Think of other ways to increase your independence.

➢ Leave money, an extra set of keys, copies of important documents and extra clothes with someone you trust so you can leave quickly.

➢ Determine who would be able to let you stay with them or lend you money. Have a safety plan, even if you think you won't need it.

➢ Keep the local shelter telephone numbers close at hand (shelters take toll calls). Know your calling card number or keep some change with you at all times for emergency telephone calls. Remember that 911 is also free from public telephone booths. Always have your cell phone handy.

➤ Plan the safest way to leave the abuser. If you have to leave, plan well, because when you do leave, the hostility may increase. But, at least you won't be there to be victimized any more.

3. Safety in your home after the abuser has left

➤ Change the locks on your doors as soon as possible. Get additional locks and safety devices to secure your windows.

➤ Discuss a safety plan with your children for when you are not with them.

➤ Inform your children's school, day care provider, etc., about who has permission to pick up your children. Unless you have an order from the courts giving you sole custody, the legal father of your children may have the same custodial rights you have, including removing your children from school or the day care facility. Don't think for a moment that he wouldn't take them; he will.

➤ If you have a restraining order, tell your neighbors and/or the landlord that your partner no longer lives with you, and tell them to call the police if they see him at your home.

4. Safety with a restraining order

➤ Keep your restraining order with you at all times. Keep a copy of it in a safe place, where the abuser cannot take it from you. Check with the local police department to make sure that they have a copy of the order.

➤ Call the police right away if the abuser breaks the restraining order. A violation of the order is a criminal offense.

➤ Ask a trusted neighbor to stay with you until the police arrive (or stay at the neighbor's house).

> Inform your family, friends, neighbors, boss and coworkers that you have a restraining order in effect. Inform your children's school or day care provider if your children are also on the order.

> Enlist the assistance of the police department so that they become proactive with your case.

A restraining order does not always work, because the abuser may feel he doesn't have to abide by the judge's wishes. You must contact everyone you can to let them know about the order. Don't allow the abuser to violate the order. Make sure that the police are taking a firm stand against the abuser.

5. Safety on the job and in public

> Decide who best to inform at your workplace about your situation; make sure that someone is informed. And that should include the office or building security people. If possible, provide a photograph of the abuser for their use.

> If possible, arrange to have someone screen your telephone calls.

> Have a safety plan for when you arrive and leave work. Have someone escort you to your car, bus or train, or perhaps ride with a co-worker. If possible, use a variety of routes to go home. Think about what you would do if something happened on the way home, whether in your car, the bus, the train, etc. Again, have a plan ready even if you think you won't need it.

6. Safety and emotional health

> Decide whom you can trust to call, and talk freely and openly to get the support you need.

> If you are thinking about returning to a potentially abusive situation, discuss an alternative plan with a trusted friend, or call the local shelter hotline number to

talk anonymously. Do not, under any set of circumstances, go back into the abusive situation; it will only get much worse. The abuser may have calmed down for a while, and he'll try to make you believe that everything is going to be alright. It will never be alright; the abuse will only escalate over time. Call your local domestic violence agency for an appointment to discuss a personal safety plan with an advocate.

➢ Think positively about yourself. Be assertive with others about your needs.

➢ Read books, articles and poems to help you feel stronger and connected.

➢ Attend a women's or victim's group to gain support from others and to learn more about yourself and your relationship.

➢ If you have to communicate with the abuser for any reason, determine the safest way to do so, such as calling from a public telephone. Do not meet with him under any circumstances. Meeting with him is never a good idea. He will very quickly try to control and manipulate you once again and, if that fails, he will strike out at you.

What to Take If You Leave

The following is a checklist of the things you will need to take when you leave:

➢ **Identification:**
- Driver's license
- Your birth certificate
- Your children's birth certificates
- Green card
- Passport
- Social Security card
- AFDC identification card

> **Other important papers:**
> - Lease or rental agreement
> - Insurance papers
> - Medical records for all your family members
> - School records
> - Work permits
> - Divorce/custody papers
> - Automobile registration and insurance

> **Financial:**
> - Money
> - Bank books
> - Checkbook

> **Practical and personal:**
> - House and car keys
> - Photographs and address book
> - Jewelry and other valuable or sentimental objects
> - Medication
> - Small, easily sold objects

It's important to gather all your paperwork together and keep it all in a safe place where the abuser is not likely to look, such as a shoe box, makeup case, garment bag, etc. Plan early and plan well. Have everything ready beforehand. Have you ever seen that movie *Sleeping with the Enemy* starring Julia Roberts? Plan as well as her character did in the movie. And, when you leave, never look back.

Chapter Nine

Crimes Against Children

In dealing with this particularly heartrending issue, I have turned to several sources for some guidance and direction, and have subsequently included much of their useful advice into one easy-to-read compendium. Those sources included Interpol, the United States Department of Justice reports on child abuse issues (Annual 2011), the Child Protection Guide, the Roberts Report for Child Abuse, and interviews and discussions with law enforcement colleagues[35]. Much of the information I gathered over the course of the last five years has been appended for this text.

Physical touching and intimacy are an integral part of building healthy relationships within the family. However, the need for physical intimacy within family relationships creates a degree of built-in vulnerability in our children unless we arm them to fend off the advances of potential molesters.

Statistics show that one in every four children will be victimized. (An even larger number of children are approached by potential abusers without success!) We've all heard some of the stories. I remember the case of one particular Catholic priest working in the Midwest. Over the course of several years this charming individual sexually molested a number of young boys. Under pressure he eventually left the church, but then I discovered much to my horror that he was working in an all-boys facility in St. Augustine, Florida.

The best means of protecting your child is to teach him or her the difference between good touches and bad touches, and what to do in case the worst happens.

How to Teach Children About Staying Safe

Here are the main points to emphasize and a suggested

---

[35] Phillip Mourea, Interpol (private conversation), Lyon, France, 2009.

United States. *Annual Report*. Washington, DC: Department of Justice, 2011. Print.

Roberts, Glennon. *Robert's Report for Child Abuse*. London: Metropolitan London Police. 1992. Print.

approach for teaching children:

> Remember, it is not your desire to create fear, hysteria or paranoia in your child, so teach in matter-of-fact terms. Just as you would instruct your child about escaping fire in the home, you need to teach them only how to escape. There is no real need to dwell on too many details of what might happen if they don't. Each child should be taught this information individually.

> Every human is the keeper of his body. We have the right to say who and how others may touch or look at our body. Good touches (those which are morally acceptable) make one feel good, safe and loved. For a child, this might include a goodnight kiss, a warm hug, being gently tickled or bounced on a parent's knee, holding hands or riding piggyback with daddy.

> Bad touches (those which are morally unacceptable) leave an uncomfortable feeling and not the feelings of love, respect and safety that good touches bring. This might include a pinch, a slap or a touch in a private area. Any place normally covered by a swimsuit is off limits for touching by anyone unless you or your spouse is present. One exception to this might be the doctor.

Teach your child to say "No!" to a bad touch, especially if it's in a private area of the body. And this is true even if it's an adult doing the touching, a relative, neighbor or family friend. Your child must know to say "No!" loudly and firmly and to get away quickly.

Your children must learn to trust you, and they must know enough to tell you immediately if someone does a bad touch. Be sure to emphasize that if someone asks them not to tell, they must always tell right away.

Promise your children that you will not be mad at them, and that if you did not understand the first time they told you, they need to keep telling you until you realize that a bad touch has happened. Sometimes children just don't have adequate words to express this and to convey the awful meaning to you. You have to understand this.

Don't just teach your child about good and bad touches once. You must periodically review the basic concepts; this is critical, and is especially true with a younger child. Please remember to carefully listen when your child talks to you. He has something to tell you, but may not know how. Listen to him very carefully.

Use this checklist to rate your child's knowledge about staying safe:

> Can your child recite his full name, address and telephone number, including the area code, city and state?

> Can your child make a long-distance telephone call? From a pay telephone? Dial direct or with operator assistance?

> Does your child know to dial 911?

> Does your child know never to enter anyone's home without your permission?

> Does your child know of any special home where they are not to enter under any circumstances?

> If separated from you in a store, would your child go to the nearest check-out clerk? Would he or she verify that the person is in fact an employee of the store?

> Would he or she go into the parking lot either alone or if encouraged by an adult?

> Does your child know to play only with friends, and to use the buddy-system?

> Does your child know that adults seldom ask for direction from children and that if approached by a car, they should never go near or get in an automobile with a stranger?

> Does your child know not to accept rides from strangers or even from acquaintances without your specific permission?

> If followed by an adult or a stranger, would your child know to proceed immediately to a place where there are other people, such as a store or a trusted neighbor's house?

➤ Would your child refuse an offer of a ride without your permission?

➤ Does your child know never to tell anyone over the telephone that they are home alone?

➤ Would your child yell "NO!" and create a scene in public if they were being subjected to bad touches or if approached by an adult for some untoward reason?

➤ Would your child immediately report to you if an adult asked them to keep a secret from you?

➤ Does your child know not to open the door to a stranger?

➤ Does your child know never to accept gifts of any kind from strangers?

Every 'No' answer indicates an area of risk for your child. It is probably a good idea to ask your children these questions in a modified form; they may need some help in understanding the questions. You have to realize this and be patient with them.

Safety Tips for Parents

Here are some good safety tips for parents to follow to help their children stay safe:

➤ Know your children's friends, and know the parents, relatives, friends and neighbors of those friends.

➤ Never leave your child unattended, ever. Never leave a child alone in a car (not even for a moment). Remember that someone with experience can break into your car in less than thirty seconds.

➤ Be involved in your child's activities.

➤ Listen when your child tells you that he or she does not want to be with someone. LISTEN to this. Direct, gentle questioning may reveal something you should know about. Your child telling you that he doesn't want to be with someone or near someone should set off all the alarm bells. LISTEN TO YOUR CHILD.

➤ Pay attention when someone shows greater-than-normal interest in your child. Find out why. Be extremely cautious in this situation. Do not allow opportunities for that adult to be with your child alone, ever.

➤ Have your child fingerprinted and know where to locate dental records.

➤ Be sensitive to changes in your child's behavior and attitudes. Be especially alert for any talk portraying premature sexual understanding. Never belittle any fear or concern on the part of your children. Avoid communicating hysteria or excessive fear for their safety.

➤ Take a photograph of your child each year (four times a year for children under two years old). Have several copies on hand in case your child turns up missing. This will greatly aid in the early stages of an investigation.

➤ If your child is missing, call the police immediately. Do not wait for even one moment; have them initiate a search right away. Those first few minutes and hours are so very critical. Give them an accurate description, including what your child is wearing. Know where your child was last seen and in whose company. Be able to provide information on any of your child's identifying characteristics. Think of those items now and write them down. It may be more difficult to concentrate in times of extreme stress.

➤ Develop a set procedure for you and your child to follow in the event that you become separated while away from home. As an example, both you and your child may call a trusted friend and leave an address and telephone number to call back, and then wait at the telephone until you're reunited. If this does not work, however, call the police immediately.

➤ Do not buy items that visibly display your child's name. It could give an abductor the advantage of seeming to know your child. ("Hey, Billy, your mom's been in an accident. We need to rush to the hospital. Jump in the car!").

➤ Be sure that your child's school or day care center will not release your child to anyone other than you or someone you officially designate.

➤ Instruct the school to contact you immediately if your child is absent, or if someone other than you arrives to pick him or her up without advance notice from you.

What to Do If You Suspect the Worst

If you suspect that your child has been molested, one expert suggests that you ask the child directly. Children rarely tell their secrets unless you ask. And they rarely make up lies indicating that they have been attacked or molested if no molestation has occurred. Try to avoid hysteria.

If your child tells you that a bad touch has occurred, be sure to get all the facts from the child as soon as possible. Be careful not to destroy any evidence. Do not allow your anger to overwhelm you. If you're angry, as you most certainly will be, be sure that your child understands that you are not mad at him. Do not take matters into your own hands. Call the police. The amount of information your child gives will probably be determined by how reasonable and unruffled you appear to be; they are directly proportional. They desperately need to trust you and your maturity at this critical time.

Be a rock for your child. Be understanding, be loving and comforting. Remember that a pedophile may try to persuade your child to not say anything to you about what happened, and your child will be terrified and confused.

Reassure your child of your love. Tell him you will not punish him and tell him he is not in trouble. Remember, even if your child has been thoughtless, careless and even willfully disobedient to your instructions that were designed to protect him or her, your child is still the victim, not a criminal. Hold out the hope for a happier time very soon.

Emphasize to your child that the offender did something wrong, and that it was not the child's fault. Call the police immediately. And also remember, from a law enforcement point of view and from the state prosecutor's position, that physical evidence may be less conclusive with the passage of time. Call the police immediately.

In cases of incest, call the law enforcement agency without delay. Failure to report a known crime such as this may make you an accomplice.

Don't confront the offender. It's the job of law enforcement to go after the vile individual who may have done something to your child. Do not take matters into your own hands.

Take your child for a complete physical examination immediately (with the knowledge of the police investigator). It will reassure him or her that there is no permanent physical damage, and may verify important physical evidence that should be turned over to the police.

Allow your child to talk about his experience at his own pace. Silencing him will not help him to forget, and forcing it will never cure him.

Get competent counseling, even if it's only for a short period of time.

Common symptoms of sexual abuse:

If you suspect the worst, look for warning signs that could indicate something terrible may have happened.

➢ Explicit (sometimes bizarre) sexual knowledge

➢ Precocious sex-related experimentation or speech

➢ Toilet training relapses

➢ Smearing of feces or urine

➢ Gagging and unexplained vomiting

➢ Speech problems

- Masturbation

- Withdrawal from normal human contact

- Stomach and head pains

- Bedwetting

- Suicidal depression, and self-destructive tendencies

- Excessive fear of selected individuals or locations

- Loss of appetite

- Unexplained bruises or injuries in genital areas

- Blood spotting or unexplained substances on underwear

- Abrupt or radical behavioral or attitude changes

- Lack of self-esteem or self-worth

- Ulcers, colitis, anorexia or other stress related disorders

- Alcohol or drug use

- Frequent nightmares

- Excessive passivity

- Vaginal or urinary tract infections

- Infections of the mouth, gums or throat.

In addition to watching for these signs, parents should be vigilant for venereal disease of the anus or throat. Such incidences are no longer uncommon in children. Parent should also be alert if any adult shows excessive attention to your child. An abuser will create occasions to be alone with your child. DO NOT ALLOW THIS. Parents should also be on the lookout for any unexplained gifts, extra money or the presence of pornography in their child's possessions.

The Importance of Supervision

All the experts with whom I have spoken agree that abuse outside of the family occurs more often when parents fail to properly supervise children. Yet for many, economic necessity seems to conflict with the responsibilities and time demands of parenting. How can one be both provider and protector? Single parents have fewer options today. They may have day care, babysitters or latchkey children.

But for married, working couples the issue may be further complicated by the question of having either one or both parents employed. "Should I work or should I stay at home?" The question is important, since the risk of out-of-family abuse increases as the supervision of children decreases.

Many parents today are asking themselves "Could I afford not to work?" And some are concluding that the cost of working outside of the home is too high, the rewards too meager, and the risks too great.

Chapter Ten

Protecting Your Child from the Internet

If you're a parent like me, you know that the most precious possession you could ever have is your children. You and I would do anything to protect our children from the evils of the world. Some of those evils, like the men who prey on children, are particularly loathsome. So, for example, if we knew where there was someone who committed acts of incest, rape, sexual assault or any other heinous crimes against children, we would definitely keep that person away from our children. Well, if you have a personal computer in your home, that very same pedophile or child pornographer could be paying them visits.

Each year there are thousands of cases of men, many of them posing as teenagers, contacting children on the Internet. They may offer your child gifts, send them sexually explicit photographs and give them the time and attention that all children crave. But for these twisted monsters, the bottom line is that they want to teach your child how to make love to somebody. They want to teach your child how to have sex. Plain and simple, that is all they have in mind. It is their common denominator. They want to have sex with your child; that's it.

The risks are the same for boys and girls. Studies have shown, however, that boys are somewhat less likely to report cases of sexual encounters. And children affected by these predators have been as young as eight or nine.

It is estimated that there are tens of thousands of websites devoted to pedophilia, and the numbers seem to be multiplying. The Supreme Court, in all its wisdom, recently struck down the Child Pornography Prevention Act. Yes folks, good news for all the child pornographers, pedophiles and purveyors of filth directed at children—the Supreme Court believes that the provisions of the act, meant only to protect our children, were "overly broad and unconstitutional." What this means is that a ban on virtual images of child pornography, as seen on the web, has been eliminated. Ruling that the First Amendment protects pornography or other sexual images that only appear to depict real children engaged in sex, anything and everything is now allowed! And, of course, the Free Speech Coalition, basically a pornographer's trade group, applauded the decision. Where we're headed with this is anyone's guess, but it doesn't look good.

Fortunately, there are also websites out there that can help us protect our children from those who would prey on them. I normally don't recommend one particular website over others, because there are a great many that have merit, but there is one in particular that stands head and shoulders above most of the others, when it comes to protecting our children. It is called Family Watch Dog, a free service that can be accessed at www.familywatchdog.us. Using information from public records, the site maintains the addresses of registered sex offenders and can help you find out if any are living near you. It's an amazing online tool, and I tip my hat to the creator. If you find that a registered sex offender is living close by, you can instantly find his or her photograph and address, as well as a list of his or her convictions. (Note that the site isn't foolproof, however. If a registered sex offender moves but does not let the authorities know where he's moved to, the new address cannot be listed.)

Some research indicates that the typical on-line predator is a middle-class white male. Some may already be involved with children because of their work or involvement in sports or recreational activities where children can be found. There is an evil sickness about these predators, and their close proximity to their victims is necessary for them to continue their activities. Computers give pedophiles that close proximity.

So, what can we do to protect our children on the Internet? We should acknowledge that personal computers are certainly useful tools and that our children should be allowed some access to them. For the sake of the children, however, we must control and monitor that access.

As I have previously stated, we have to bear the responsibility for protecting and caring for our children. If we can monitor the playground to keep our children safe in that environment (and those playgrounds do, indeed, need to be monitored) we can certainly monitor the access they have to the Internet.

You must always remember that your child is just a few keystrokes away from absolute filth, hatred, violence and sexual exploitation. In one moment your child could be finding information for a school science project, and in the next moment he or she could be exposed to a pedophile's e-mail, or even looking at sexually graphic images sent by the pedophile.

Pedophiles online have instant access to innocent children. They can hide behind a benign-sounding screen name and begin a relationship with your child. That screen name, by the way, gives them a great sense of anonymity. They may be afraid of getting caught, but their need to dominate, to control and ultimately to violate your child in a more direct way overrides that fear. And if one of them does develop a relationship with your child, sooner or later he will want to meet the child. Make no mistake: the purpose for the meeting is for sex. This happens more often than you may want to believe. Pedophiles are unbelievably sick monsters, and it is up to us to form the first line of defense against this horrific epidemic, and stop the bastards in their tracks.

Guidelines to Protect Your Child on the Internet

First and foremost, you need to monitor your child's online activity: literally stand next to your child when he or she is one that computer. Be firm with this; make it the rule of the house. If your child wants to use the computer, that's fine, but you must monitor this activity.

Now, obviously, you don't have to stand there for the next three hours while your child works on a school project, but you must monitor the activity every thirty minutes or so. Here are some other things you can do:

> If an e-mail program is being used, scan the senders' addresses to find out who is contacting your child. You can even type in the child's name into a search engine to find out exactly what is being said on websites and message boards.

> Make sure that your child never reveals any personal information to any stranger who is on-line.

> Do not allow your child to have access to credit card information. With a credit card number, anything and everything imaginable is for sale on the Internet.

> ➢ Become actively involved with the operation of the computer. Use filters or parental controls to bar access to content that could be offensive or dangerous. Computer monitors will tell you where your child has been on the Internet. America On-line, as an example, offers a kids-only account that blocks children's access from all but pre-screened sites and monitored (full-time) chat rooms.

Your involvement with your children must be bold and forthright. Let them know about your concerns, and let them know that even though they may not be completely happy with the arrangement, you will be checking. No one ever said that being a parent was easy. At times it's downright difficult, but your children's safety is of paramount importance. And who bought that computer, anyway? Your child gets limited and monitored access, period.

Commercial filters like Surfwatch, Cyber Patrol, Net Nanny, CYBERsitter, and others can help to screen out some offensive websites that offer explicit information about hate and violence, alcohol and tobacco, bomb-building, Satanism and other cults, as well as the sexually explicit garbage that has become so pervasive.

What to do If You Discover a Problem

If you find out that your child has had, or is having contact with someone whom you suspect is a pedophile, immediately contact the police. If the police do not have a unit that handles these crimes, and many law enforcement agencies do not have these specialized units for this type of investigation, contact the Federal Bureau of Investigation right away. The FBI does, indeed, investigate these types of crimes and will be more than happy to assist you. The FBI is trained to deal with varieties of issues like this. There trained agents are completely nonintrusive and will protect your child. And remember, the sooner an investigation is started, the sooner the pedophile can be taken out of circulation.

Computers are wonderful devices, but our children are priceless. You must be firm, and you must control the access given to your child.

If you or your child finds a questionable website, be sure to write down the Uniform Resource Locator (URL) to report it accurately. If you and your child experience e-mail problems, save the offending messages and forward them to your Internet service provider. If you or your family is threatened in any way, contact the law enforcement agency in your area as soon as possible. If you suspect or see evidence of illegal activity on-line, seek help immediately. The following list can help you report that activity:

1. CyberTipLine/National Center for Missing and Exploited Children (800) 843-5678; www.missingkids.com/cybertip

2. United States Customs Service, (800) BE-ALERT; www.customs.ustreas.gov; e-mail of icpicc@customs.treas.gov

3. Federal Bureau of Investigation, (202) 324-3000; www.fbi.gov

4. Bureau of Alcohol, Tobacco and Firearms; www.atf.treas.gov

5. United States Drug Enforcement Administration; www.usdoj.gov/dea/

6. United States Postal Inspection Service; www.usps.gov/websites/depart/inspect/

7. Cyberangels; www.cyberangels.org

8. The Children's Partnership; www.childrenspartnership.org

9. The FBI's Parent Guide to Internet Safety; www.fbi.gov/library/pguide.htm

10. The FBI's Safety Tips for Kids on the Internet; www.fbi.gov/kids/crimepre/Internet.htm

11. GetNetWise; www.getnetwise.org

And one other thing before we continue: the world of virtual reality has taken on a whole new dimension that poses threats to your children not only on the Internet, but also in the form of computer games. Recently, while at a friend's house in Newport, Rhode Island, was introduced to a new virtual-reality computer game. The player — you or your child — has a hand controller and moves a person around on the screen. The person is an assassin. The more people this assassin can kill, the more babies in prams and police officers he can run over, the more cars he can hijack, the more people he can murder on the street or wherever else he finds them, the more points he gets. The figures on the screen appear very real. The blood gushing from gaping wounds appears real. I noticed that as this was being played out, some players were being swept up in the excitement of what was happening on the screen. And these were adults. What can this do to the mind of a child? While the game can't be sold directly to minors yet, it will certainly end up in their hands.

Virtual reality, whether it's on the Web or on a computer game on the television, can look very real, thanks to advances in technology. It doesn't matter anymore whether it's pornography or mayhem; your child will be viewing it and believing it to be real.

Chapter Eleven

Crimes Against the Elderly

It's been estimated that nationally one in every seventeen people over the age of sixty is in some way victimized each year in the United States, and that only one in every fourteen cases of elder abuse is ever reported[36]. Those figures are staggering, and the numbers are climbing.

The population is getting older, and the chances for abuse of the elderly increases daily. The enormous post-World War II baby-boomer population will soon be in the elder category. Within 15 to 20 years, many people from that generation will be entering some sort of care-provided facility or assisted-living arrangement.

The older the population becomes, the easier it is to exploit and victimize people. Statistically speaking, crimes motivated by economic gain include robbery and personal theft, as well as the household crimes of larceny, burglary and motor vehicle theft. Like the general population, elders are most susceptible to household crimes and least susceptible to violent crimes, according to figures released by the United States Department of Justice's Bureau of Justice Statistics.

Unlike younger victims of violence, however, elder victims of violence are just as likely to be robbed as they are to be assaulted. Thirty-eight percent to nearly 44 percent of the violent crimes against elders are categorized as either armed robberies or strong-armed robberies. (Armed robberies are committed with weapons such as guns and knives, etc., and strong-armed robberies are committed with fists and feet and intimidation or threat of impending violence.)

When I read these statistics and attend the briefings and meetings, I have to constantly remind myself that we are not really grasping the full picture here. The tragic reality is that no matter what those statistics say, violence and crime in general, directed against our older population, is increasing each year. And just as an aside, it's important to note that the Bureau of Justice Statistics gleans its reportable figures from select law enforcement agencies across the

---

[36] United States. Department of Justice. *Elderly Exploitation and Abuse*. Washington, DC: Bureau of Justice Statistics, 2011. Print.

United States. Those particular figures are extremely subjective in nature because the reporting systems change nearly every year. So, as an example, for last year, what was narrowly defined as a strong-armed robbery against someone age sixty or older could this year be considered theft (because some genius in the government changed the rules to make certain crimes easier to swallow, probably because of politics).

I also remind myself that the folks at the Bureau of Justice Statistics are more or less accountants, have never seen or investigated one victim of elderly abuse, and are the same group of really very nice people who labeled certain really bad crimes "household" crimes, as if that makes them insignificant. I look at all those reports with a jaundiced eye, knowing full well that our elder population is being victimized more each day. No matter how you change the labels or move the figures around, it doesn't take a genius to see through all the nonsense.

Most victims of violent crime are attacked by a stranger rather than by a relative or someone whom the victim knows. Robbery victims age sixty-five or older are much more likely than younger victims to be particularly vulnerable to offenders they do not know. Half of the elderly victims of violence, and a quarter of those under age sixty-five, are victimized at or near their home. The vulnerability of the elderly to violent crime at or near their home may reflect their lifestyle. Often living alone and not working away from home, people age sixty-five or older are also less likely than younger people to go out after dark to social gatherings.

Public opinion surveys conducted over the course of the last twenty-five years among national samples of people age fifty or older consistently show that about half of those people feel afraid to walk alone at night in their own neighborhoods.

Elder abuse knows no boundaries. It occurs in every city and town in the country, and its victims are wealthy, poor, well-educated and illiterate, healthy and sick, men and women. It is often a "family issue." In many cases, spouses, parents, children and other relatives are the abusers. It occurs when a caregiver or family member mistreats, neglects or exploits a person age sixty or older.

What is Elder Abuse?

Elder abuse can include any of the following:

➢ Physical, such as pushing or hitting;

➢ Psychological with frequent yelling, intimidation, demeaning or threatening behavior;

➢ Neglect, where medical care, personal care, nutrition, compassion or other needed services are withheld; and,

➢ Exploitation, where someone or some people are living off of an elder's income or assets without his or her consent.

I have been witness to hundreds of these cases, and I know as I write this that there are many thousands of unreported cases involving criminal enterprise against our elderly population occurring right at this moment.

The variety of crimes perpetrated against the elderly population makes your head swim. In general, the elderly are viewed by criminals as easy targets. I remember an interview I conducted at a prison facility in Northern Virginia right outside of Washington, D.C. The convicted burglar, armed robber and murderer, thirty-eight years of age, freely told me that he had picked out victims who were "old" because they offered little or no resistance, didn't hear or see that well, and usually had "more money and stuff" than younger victims. Over the course of about 20 years, this convict had burglarized close to 70 homes (the exact figure probably will never be known), robbed and beaten dozens of elderly victims, and murdered at least one. He said that he broke into their homes because they usually went to bed early, had their hearing aids out or the television on extra loud. He could be in and out of their house and they would never realize he had been there. And, even if he was discovered, he would simply batter the elderly victim or knock them to the floor and leave.

Another type of criminal activity that targets our older population are frauds and scams, such as those discussed in the next chapter. Part of the reason they are being targeted is that they come from a generation of people who actually trusted others and took people at their word.

Recognizing Abuse

The abuse of the elderly can be difficult to identify because the perpetrators try to hide their crime, and victims tend to explain it away or deny it. The following are some, but not all, of the signs that could indicate an elderly person is being abused:

➢ Bruises, cuts or bumps

➢ Depression

➢ Little or no money

➢ Vague or continuous health complaints

➢ Complete dependence on the caregiver

➢ Fear of the caregiver

These signs could indicate that family members are the abusers:

➢ Substance abuse

➢ Sudden affluence of the family-member caregiver

➢ Bursts of anger

➢ Fatigue

➢ Aggressive or defensive behavior

➢ Complete dependence on the elder

Abuse by Caregivers

When our elderly family members go into nursing homes, or have some sort of caregiver taking over the daily tasks to keep them healthy, functioning and vital, we are really taking an awful lot for granted. Our assumptions are that they are being well taken care of and are having all their needs adequately met. But is that really always the case?

Statistics show that elder abuse at the hands of caregivers is also on the rise. Now, one out of every eleven people who are under the direct supervision of a caregiver of some kind is being either physically or psychologically abused, significantly neglected in same fashion or exploited for their assets. It is absolutely amazing. When we consider that many cases of elder abuse are in fact never reported, and then also understand that the former figure of one out of every eleven is a conservative figure, we shortly arrive at a probably more accurate accounting of one out of ten — one-tenth of our elderly population!

Some Case Studies About Caregivers

These are three scenarios that were taken from files of actual cases (their names have been changed here):

1. James and Virginia Govens lived in Daytona Beach, Florida, near the Atlantic Ocean. James was 81 years old and was restricted to a wheelchair. He could talk about general subjects, but had a memory problem. His wife, Virginia, was legally blind and bedridden, and couldn't remember things too well, either. Both were in need of a caregiver, but the last one stole their credit cards and went on a shopping spree at the Volusia Mall in town. Nancy, a new caregiver, had stepped in. She took good care of the Govenses. Within the year, the Govenses' family doctor and therapist were fired by Nancy. Nancy became the beneficiary of both the Govenses' new will and their estate, valued at $500,000.00. She took ownership of their beautiful house by quit claim deed, and her name was added to all the Govens' bank accounts. Nancy received a $20,000 loan from the Govenses to buy the nursing service from a person named Dorothy. But, Nancy didn't tell the couple that she, in fact, was "Dorothy," who already owned the business.

    James became sweet towards Nancy. Virginia stayed in her bed. Virginia didn't like the new doctor and missed her physical therapist. Because of her blindness, Virginia had no idea that she had signed a new will and a quit claim deed.

Finally, Nancy hired Consuela as a home companion for the Govenses. Consuela befriended the elderly couple and eventually refused to sidetrack their mail to Nancy, even though Nancy insisted. Nancy fired Consuela, but when Consuela went to Virginia's bed to say goodbye, Virginia asked her to call the police for help. Consuela went to the police, and a month later Nancy was arrested for exploitation and grand theft.

2. Donna Livingston was eighty-six years old and lived alone in her nice house on the Halifax River in Florida. She suffered from Organic Brain Syndrome (OBS), so a longtime family friend handled her assets.

    Buzz, the mailman, visited Donna just about every day. Donna often invited Buzz in and gave him some beer or lunch. One day, an attorney named Valerie came to Donna's house with Buzz. Donna signed a new will, giving Buzz both her home and her assets. On another day, Donna signed over power of attorney to Buzz, and his name was added to all her bank accounts. Poor Donna couldn't remember anything, but her longtime friend found out about the situation and complained to the postal inspector. The postal inspector subsequently went to the police, and two months later Buzz was arrested for exploitation and grand theft.

3. Janet was eighty-two years old and lived alone in her house in Fairfax, Virginia. Janet also suffered from OBS and was incapacitated. Although she could move short distances with a walker, the neighbors usually brought her the morning paper because they plainly saw her lack of mobility.

    One day, a "nice man" named Matthew knocked on Janet's door and told her that she had a beautiful home. Matthew started mowing her lawn and, believe it or not, eventually became her caregiver. Janet became very dependent on Matthew because her memory was very short and she couldn't physically care for herself.

Eventually, Janet signed over her $300,000 home to Matthew with a quit claim deed. On another day, Matthew's name was added to all her bank accounts and certificates of deposit. Finally, Matthew cashed in the CDs, withdrew all the money from the bank accounts and even took out a home equity loan on his newly acquired Fairfax property.

Shortly after this, Matthew left the state on vacation for a few weeks without providing a substitute caregiver for Janet. Several days after he left, the neighbors heard Janet's moans coming from inside the house. Out of concern they called the police. The police responded and, after breaking into the house, found Janet lying on the kitchen floor covered with ants.

At the hospital, Janet was diagnosed as having severe dehydration, acute psychosis and broken ribs. The doctor believed that she had fallen and been left on the floor for several days. An old friend of Janet's heard that she was in the hospital and decided to call the police to let them know about Matthew. Upon Matthew's return to Fairfax, he was arrested for exploitation of the elderly, grand theft and felony elderly neglect. Janet died a short time later.

If the above three scenarios seem a bit out of the ordinary, you should understand that they are in fact actually quite common types of occurrences. For those people who have elderly family members living alone, or under the supervision of some type of caregiver, it is vital that you and your family remain active in the daily oversight of both the caregiver and of course, the elderly relative.

Preventative Measures

It's not enough to just take the word of a caregiver that everything's alright, or that the elder patient is being well taken care of. These are my suggestions if you have an elderly relative in need of care:

➢ Have a family meeting. If possible, include your elderly relative in that meeting. They should be made to feel as if they are a vital, integral part of the decision making process (because they are).

➢ Do not include the caregiver in any meetings such as this.

➢ During the course of the meeting, be completely forthright with the elderly relative regarding suspicions you may have about the qualifications and genuineness of the caregiver.

➢ Voice general concerns about what could take place. You may want to refer to this book or other studies that describe the ways in which the elderly can be taken advantage of. Do not hold back your feelings about this.

➢ Make pointed suggestions that your elderly relative should allow only certain family members to assist in the oversight of his or her assets. In many cases the relative will stubbornly resist this, but sometimes it's much better to take the lead. If you do meet this resistance, try the direct approach: "This is what we're going to do."

➢ Have your elderly relative's financial matters taken care of now. The will and the Power of Attorney should be reviewed and completed as soon as possible. Naming an executor to the estate is advisable. Don't wait on these types of issues until someone is unfortunately not able to knowingly (with complete understanding) sign the necessary documents. Someone with dementia, as an example, may not have the capacity to understand what is going on six months down the road. Make sure that the legal documents are kept in a secure location, such as a safety deposit box.

➤ If there is insurance paperwork or policies in effect, gather them up, as well. To file an insurance claim on someone's life, you don't necessarily need the actual documents, but the insurance companies do request that they be returned with the completed claim form and death certificate. If they're not available, that's fine, but having them at your disposal is extremely helpful.

➤ Also, collect any and all medical records, checks or any bank records or paperwork and quit claim deeds, or the applications for a deed.

➤ Do not allow caregivers, no matter who they are, to have any access to your elderly relative's financial records or documents, assets including available cash, or even someone's valued property, such as jewelry.

➤ If your relative is in a nursing care facility of some sort, you and your family must become actively involved in the checking and the oversight of that facility as it pertains to the care of your loved one. My suggestion would be that each person in the family be assigned certain days and times when they can pay unexpected visits to the facility. Keep the facility off balance. Don't tell them ahead of time when you will visit. Just show up as often as possible. The more the visits that your loved one receives, the better care that he or she gets. It's just that simple.

➤ Remember the obvious signs to look for when someone is being neglected and/or abused. Every time you're there, check for those signs.

> If you suspect that a home health aide, residential care giver or a nursing facility is abusing, neglecting or exploiting your elderly relative in any way, report your suspicions to the police right away. We all live hectic, busy lives and sometimes we don't know whether we're coming or going. And we all have relatives, perhaps siblings, who don't want to get involved or just don't seem to care, or they become involved and controlling for all the wrong reasons. But if your mother or father is the person lying day after day in a nursing home, you have an obligation to take the time to visit—if not on a daily basis, then at least once in a while.

While conducting some research in Maine, I associated myself with a nursing home for about a year. During that time, I provided assistance as a medical technician, but I also gained a great deal of information for this book. And I lost count of the number of instances of abuse. Patients were crammed into rooms with inadequate furnishings. Their sheets and bedding were left unchanged and unwashed for long periods of time. Some of them were not cleaned or didn't have their undergarments washed for periods of time. Many were left to sit in urine-soaked or soiled underwear.

The food was inadequate and of poor quality. The bananas they were provided, as an example, were rotting and should have been thrown out rather than given to the residents. In addition, the residents were not given enough to drink. Their money, if left lying about, was stolen by certain staff members.

Patients were left to sit for hour upon hour with absolutely no stimulus whatsoever. Many residents were handled roughly, and certainly without any care or concern. At least two of the medical staff had drug problems and stole from the residents or the medical lockers. The list goes on and on, and this was just one facility out of hundreds in the state of Maine. It was actually listed as one of the better places to have your elderly family member live!

After a full year of investigations, during which I went behind the backs of the staff and took extra measures to ensure the safety of the residents, and had meetings with family members who never realized the extent of the abuse in that facility, the office for the attorney general finally got involved and the facility was closed down. One staff member was arrested, and she's now serving a lengthy prison term. The residents were fortunately moved elsewhere.

Don't think for a moment that it can't happen to you and your family. It can, and it does every day. A certain family member may take over as the Power of Attorney (POA). Your elderly father, as an example, may go along with it thinking that certainly nothing bad would happen to him. But as his health deteriorates, you begin to see that the POA has now started to take control of your father's finances. No matter what the will might read, the POA might convince your father to sign a codicil to the original will, and that codicil now gives all the assets to the POA alone. Your father may have signed the codicil because his dementia prevented him from understanding what it was he was signing. When your father dies, all the assets could go to the POA.

Here's something else that could — and does — happen all too often:

Before your father dies, the POA could convince your father to move to someplace like Las Vegas, promising all sorts of things, including daily visits by the POA and his girlfriend. It is all a lie of course; there are no visits or anything else. The move to Las Vegas removes your father from familiar settings, from his family and friends, and from their daily visits. And the move also isolates your father and makes him completely dependent upon the POA for everything.

What can be done at this point? Well, truthfully, not too much. Your father has been exploited, and once in Las Vegas (and I'm only using Las Vegas as an example, but it could be anywhere away from the family influence), he was neglected. The family member (the POA) is a thief, and one of the lowest forms of humanity known, but he's free and clear with your father's assets. *Don't let this progress to the point where it becomes impossible to do anything about it!* Call the attorney general's office; get law enforcement involved; call the district attorney's office. Do everything in your power to stop what is happening! When your father dies, it's too late.

This situation actually happened in my family and to my father. These types of things happen every day.

A Final Word

Some types of elder abuse can be prevented. There are steps that can be taken to protect yourself or your family member from abuse.

For the elder:

> ➢ Stay in touch with your friends. Make new friends through your senior center or community organization.

> ➢ Stay active, exercise, volunteer, take some classes at the local college or university or start a new hobby.

> ➢ Keep accurate records of your bank accounts and assets.

> ➢ Plan for long-term care. Make out a will and advance health-care directives.

For family members:

> ➢ Keep in contact with your aging relatives.

> ➢ Encourage your elder relatives to live as independently as possible.

> ➢ Familiarize yourself with community resources such as transportation, meals, homemakers, respite and adult-care facilities.

Chapter Twelve

Frauds and Scams

When it comes to the crimes of frauds and scams, I've got to tell you that as stupid as many criminals are, they have absolutely no lack of imagination. I've often thought that if they could harness and redirect all that energy, imagination and savoir-faire into good, positive works, this world would be such a wonderful place to live. And, they would probably all be terribly wealthy, as well. But, of course, God gave us the ability to make choices in our lives and, human nature being what it is, for whatever reason, a certain percentage of the world's population figures that they are just plain entitled to everyone else's property, like it or not.

That imagination on the part of the pariahs of the world often translates into the crimes of frauds and scams. According to the Random House Dictionary of the English Language (the unabridged edition), fraud is "deceit, trickery, sharp practice, or breach of confidence, used to gain some unfair or dishonest advantage.[37]"

Frauds and scams are used to swindle people out of their money and/or property. That's basically it. That's the bottom line for the criminal—he wants your money. And he's going to cheat you out of it using any of a variety of sometimes really imaginative schemes.

The way these lovelies go about cheating us out of our money is truly mind-boggling. Their approaches vary, but initially you can be contacted either through an unsolicited telephone call, through a mailer such as a postcard advertisement, through a direct contact such as someone coming to your door, and even on the street, such as when you're at the mall or shopping, or anywhere else you can imagine.

Telemarketing Scams

Regarding the unsolicited telephone call, according to the Federal Bureau of Investigation, at least 14,000 illegal telemarketing operations are going on in the United States each day[38]. Here's what you should

---

[37] Flexner, Stuart Berg. *Random House Dictionary of the English Language (unabridged edition)*, New York: Random House, 2012. Print.

[38] United States. *Statistical Analysis - 2010*. Washington, DC: Federal Bureau of Investigation, 2010. Print.

know:

- ➢ Illegal telemarketing is just that, it's illegal and it's a crime.

- ➢ Forty billion dollars are lost, swindled from good, honest people in the U.S. each year because of telemarketers.

- ➢ The tone of voice of the caller, or their seeming demeanor, does not mean that they are not criminals. Some of them can sound pretty convincing, but they are all indeed criminals.

- ➢ Legitimate companies will never pressure you into doing something that you rationally would want to think about beforehand. Illegal telemarketers will often use pressure tactics.

- ➢ It is illegal to require money up front in order to be eligible for a prize or even to enter a contest. The criminals will often use the approach that a sum of money is needed to place your name, as an example, among the finalists in a contest. Or perhaps they may need shipping or handling costs, or insurance costs, before your "prize" can be sent.

- ➢ Legitimate companies can always provide literature for you to review before any possible decisions are made. Fraudulent companies will usually refuse to send you anything.

- ➢ If you give any amount of money to an illegal telemarketer, you will never see that money again.

- ➢ If you are approached in this manner, even with a telephone call, report it to the police. You can also contact the National Fraud Information Center at (800) 876-7060.

Warning Signs of Scams

It's important for everyone, especially senior citizens, to be on the lookout for telemarketing scams. Here are some warning signs:

- ➢ When anyone is asked for payments, for prizes or money ahead of time, it's fraud and it's a crime. Call the police.

- ➢ A telemarketer may ask you (pressure you) to take the offer immediately or "miss the opportunity." Know that this is fraud.

- ➢ If the caller refuses to send you anything in the mail that you can review at your leisure, it is fraud.

- ➢ If anyone claims that you can make a huge profit in an investment opportunity (scheme) with little or no risk, just remind yourself that all investments are risky. (In my opinion, the only investment in this life where there is no risk, and all reward, is our relationship with God. Now that's what you call a safe bet.)

- ➢ If the caller asks for a donation, refuse. Only donate your hard-earned money to a very few trusted charities, and only those where you have not been approached by some unknown voice on the telephone. That's fraud, and it's illegal.

- ➢ If a caller insists that the money you're sending in must be picked up by private courier, know again that you're dealing with a fraudulent situation and people are trying to take advantage of you. Call the police to report this. Also, let your relatives know what's going on. They may be able to help you.

- ➢ If they ask for your money by wire transfer, again it's illegal. Call the police.

- ➢ If they ask for cash, credit-card information or your Social Security number, do not give them any of this information — it's illegal for them to ask. Hang up and call the police right away.

- ➢ If callers are relentless and keep calling you, even after you told them not to call, that's illegal. Hang up on them and call the police.

➢ If the caller claims to represent a company offering to get you a loan, credit or even credit cards to repair a bad debt, it's a scam, it's illegal, and you should call the police. And you can tell them that you're calling the police.

➢ If someone offers to get money back for you that you previously lost to another scam, for an up-front fee of course, they're trying to scam you yet again. Please, call the police.

➢ If the company has a name that is intended to sound like a government agency or any well-known company, it's a scam.

➢ If the telemarketer acts as if he or she has done business with you before, use caution. More than likely they're lying to you and it's fraud.

➢ In addition to asking the caller for literature, ask for a list of references. If they refuse to supply a list, know that you're talking with a criminal.

➢ If the caller asks for your calling card number as identification for purchases, or for identification purposes (they use both variations), refuse to give any information, and call the police.

➢ If someone claims that you've won a prize, and you don't remember entering any contests, it's a scam. Even if you have entered a contest, be very careful of what is being said on the telephone.

As I mentioned in the preceding chapter, there are frauds and scams that target the elderly. Here are some warning signs to watch for. An elderly person could be a target if:

➢ He receives an inordinate amount of junk mail for contests, free trips, prizes and sweepstakes, etc.

- He receives frequent calls from strangers offering great money-making opportunities or asking for charitable contributions.

- He is making repeated large payments to out-of-state or international (even off-shore) companies or institutions; he or she could be a target.

- He is having payments picked up by private courier.

- He receives lots of cheap items, such as costume jewelry, small appliances, pens and pencils, beauty products, water filters, etc.

- He receives a "great deal" on a burial plot.

- He receives an offer for life insurance coverage above and beyond what he may already have, or an offer of term insurance where the premium paid for the coverage "will never increase for the life of the coverage."

These are but a few of the warning signs of fraud. As we previously discussed, you must become involved in the oversight of your elderly relative. If any of the aforementioned scenarios sounds familiar to you, make sure you investigate. More than likely it's fraud.

Fraud via Phone Cards and Phone Calls

If you make a call from a public telephone, be careful. Many criminals will linger close by because they want to hear you tell someone your Social Security number, credit card number and information, your calling card number or anything else that they can use. Watch for people around you. You can also block the view of the keypad while entering credit card or calling card numbers, and speak directly into the mouthpiece in a quiet voice. Regarding the calling cards, you may want to find a public telephone that has the card swipe mechanism. It instantly reads the calling card number magnetically.

By the way, your calling card number is like money in the bank to these criminals, who can use it to sell long-distance calls to locations around the world. If they're not loitering close by you at a public telephone, someone may call you at home posing as a telephone company representative and ask for your calling card number to either check on unauthorized charges or to help "trap a telephone scam artist." Don't give any information to anyone.

In addition, never accept toll charges for third-party calls. Here's how that scam usually goes: someone may call claiming to be a representative of the telephone company. The caller requests your help in an investigation by asking you to say "yes" when an operator calls to verify third-party charges (for toll calls made by someone else and charged to your number) for a specific period of time. You're assured that you won't be charged for these calls. If, however, you hesitate or seem reluctant to cooperate, the caller may say that your telephone service will be terminated, or that you'll have to pay for all fraudulent calls charged to your telephone. This is a pretty common scheme, and you should know that these types of calls do not originate from the telephone company. You should report this to the police, and perhaps to that telephone company.

If callers or mailings offer products and prizes when all you have to do is call an 800 number or what appears to be a regular telephone number, be careful. If you call, you may be asked to give an identification number, such as your Social Security number, or perhaps accept a collect call. In either instance you will be billed. The same is true for 900 numbers. Remember not to give out any information at all to anyone; don't believe for a minute that a prize is awaiting you. It's another scam.

A pretty recent addition to the laundry list of scams is the investment-counselor caller with the too-good-to-be-true investment deals, the precious metals and time share, or vacation package deals. They're all worthless; they will all take your money in some fashion and they are all illegal.

International Scams

According to Greg Farrell of *USA Today* in a report about a new wave of scam activity, many criminals (scam artists) are operating from other countries and targeting Americans. He wrote, "Don't take candy from strangers, especially if the candy arrives in the form of a check for $80,000.[39]"

---

[39] Farrell, Greg. "Corporate Crooks." *USA Today*. December 11, 2007. Print.

That's the same message from the U.S. Postal Inspection Service, which is sounding the alarm over a recent rash of attempted scams aimed at defrauding people by infiltrating their bank accounts. According to Postal Inspector John Wisniewski, a ring of con artists recently tried to defraud five customers of National City Bank[40]. Wisniewski and the Secret Service are concerned over a recent uptick in similar attempts to sucker affluent Americans.

The game was simple: The con artists called some of National City's Pittsburgh-area customers, mostly retirees, and informed them that they were beneficiaries of a recent class-action settlement of an unspecified nature. The scammers then sent each individual a check from $80,000 to $100,000, drawn on an account at the Bank of Montreal. Recipients were told more money would be coming if they agreed to send out part of the money to the law firm that helped win the judgment. (Is this beginning to sound familiar?) Executives at National City noticed the unusual sizes of the deposits and checked with the Bank of Montreal. All of the checks were forgeries. Elias Bookert, age seventy-nine, a McKeesport, Pennsylvania retiree, said he was suspicious from the start. "I didn't feel right about this amount of money," he said. "I'm not the type to jump at anything real quick." Bookert took his check to National City for examination.

Fifth Third bank in Cincinnati recently uncovered a similar fraud scheme. According to Darrin Steinmann, a fraud inspector at the bank, a Nigerian-based gang scammed two people using forged checks that appeared to come from a Cincinnati-based company.

The Cincinnati scam involved an insidious twist: the perpetrators got the victims to reveal their account numbers and promised to wire funds into their accounts. Once they received those numbers, they sent the forged checks directly to their bank accounts, with forged endorsement signatures and the instruction, "for deposit only," written on the back. When the customers learned that money had been deposited into their accounts, they mistakenly believed it had been wired in, and agreed to wire most of it back out to destinations in London and Nigeria. When it was learned that the checks deposited in their own accounts were forged, they were still liable for the payments they wired out. Fifth Third Bank was able to freeze one transfer, worth $100,000 after it arrived in Nigeria. But in the other case, a New Jersey resident wired $163,000 of $175,000 out of the country and is currently

---

[40] John Wisniewski, U.S. Postal Inspection Service (statement). 2009.

on the hook for the entire sum.

If you thought that those cases are somewhat unusual or on the fringe, think again. More often than not, these types of clever scams are being perpetrated on an ever-increasing basis. They are extremely difficult to prosecute due to the fact that places such as Nigeria, and many other Third World locations, are less than forthcoming in their information-gathering and enforcement efforts. Nigeria is in the midst of a near civil war, and terrorists roam the countryside. What little law enforcement there is in the country is either corrupt from top to bottom or completely inept.

It's been repeated a thousand times by law enforcement officials all over the world: "Something that is too good to be true, is." If you are ever the recipient of something like this, call the police. In reference to notices of class action lawsuits, if you receive something indicating that you may be involved as a possible benefactor of a class action law suit, use caution. At the very least, call the company or organization that is being sued. Affirm that there really is a law suit. More than likely there's no class action law suit at all. If, on the other hand, you receive a check such as the ones described, call the police. It's nothing more than another case of fraud.

Identity Theft and Credit

Identity theft is no joke. Consider this scenario: a businesswoman's Social Security number is stolen and an awful nightmare follows. The thief runs to another state and uses the woman's identity to obtain a new driver's license and several credit cards, and then runs up a slew of charges. As a result, the woman, who had an impeccable credit history, is denied a mortgage, and it will take many months to straighten the mess out. These thieves are seldom caught and, even if caught, the attempt to prosecute them is extremely difficult. Attempting to prove a case against them, especially when some elements of the crime may have occurred in another state, is almost impossible.

One victim had to contact the three major credit bureaus in order to give them a code that creditors would have to know before issuing any new charges on her account. And the situation could have indeed been much worse for this particular victim because the credit bureaus are extremely difficult to reach.

The credit bureaus, Equifax, Experion and Trans Union have a history of placing callers on hold for protracted periods of time. And if you're not on hold, a voice may tell you that "all our representatives are busy assisting other customers." As an experiment, I tried calling each of the bureaus and was placed on hold every time. After waiting a full eight minutes with Equifax, I was told by that voice to call back at a later time. The credit bureaus have to be reached, but getting through to someone is an exercise in frustration.

According to the Federal Trade Commission, the credit bureaus must answer their calls within three-and-a-half minutes, and 90 percent of consumers are supposed to be connected with a live person without getting a busy signal[41]. Good luck; it's been my experience that the FTC guidelines are seldom followed.

By the way, if you have done everything you can and the three credit bureaus still have not answered your calls or responded to your needs in a timely manner, you can write a letter of complaint to the Federal Trade Commission. This last recourse usually produces quick, positive results.

The address is:

Federal Trade Commission
Consumer Response Center - FCRA
Washington, D.C. 20580

How to Prevent It

Here's what to do to prevent yourself from becoming a victim of these crimes:

➢ Do not carry any extra credit cards, your Social Security number, passport or birth certificate in your wallet or handbag.

➢ Never throw credit card or ATM receipts in the trash. You should shred all of these items.

---

[41] Leibowitz, Jon and Vladeck, David. *The Federal Trade Commission's Consumer Guidelines.* Washington, DC: Federal Trade Commission, 2010. Print.

➢ Check your monthly bills and statements for any unusual credit charges that were not authorized.

➢ Shred any and all pre-approved credit offers that come in the mail, unless, of course, you actually want one of them.

➢ Be on the lookout for any strange credit card statements in your name that you never applied for.

➢ Obtain a copy of your credit report from the three credit bureaus every year. Check those reports for any unauthorized charges and for who made inquiries into your file. The credit bureaus may have differing information about your credit history, and they update their files every three, six or twelve months.

➢ Immediately report any crime to the police and report any missing or stolen credit cards to the card issuers. Call the fraud protection units at the three credit bureaus' special telephone numbers:

Equifax: (800) 270-3435; www.equifax.com

Experion: (800) 397-3742; www.experion.com

Trans Union: (800) 680-7289; www.trans-union.com

➢ Write letters to the three bureaus demanding that they notify you by mail or by telephone before they issue any more credit in your name. Also let them know that you want a "promotional block" put on your credit file. This prevents them from giving your private information to any other party. You also have the right to insert a 100-word statement of your own choosing into your personal file.

➢ Tell the three bureaus to add a fraud statement to your file which requires any potential creditor to contact you for your approval before issuing any and all credit applications in your name. And you have the right to obtain all the names of any recent inquiries or credit accounts that may be new to your file.

- If your checks are stolen, notify the bank and get a new card, and change your account number as well as your password if you use an ATM card.

- Never include Social Security numbers on personal checks.

- If your Social Security number has been stolen, contact the Social Security Administration and have them issue you a new card with a new number. You should do this as soon as possible.

- If you suspect mail theft, in addition to filing a report with the police, you should contact the postal inspector for your area.

- Install a locked mailbox at your residence.

- Do not leave paid bills in the mailbox for the carrier to pick up. Take them to the post office.

- Pick up your new checks at the bank. Do not have them mailed.

- Cancel all unused credit cards.

- Carry only a very few credit cards.

- Never write down PIN numbers or passwords. Memorize them instead. Do not use part of your Social Security number or other easy to guess words or numbers.

- Never allow sales clerks to write down your credit card numbers on your checks for additional information.

- Call the credit card company if your card has expired and you have not received a new one.

According to Jean Sherman Chatzky, in an article entitled "How to Foil Identity Thieves," "Identity theft — using someone else's Social Security number to obtain credit cards or funds from bank accounts — is on the rise, says the Federal Trade Commission. In late summer, it reported that the number of calls to its identity theft hotline (1-877-IDTHEFT) had doubled since March, to more than 800 calls per week.[42]"

I checked, and those figures are now around 1,400 per week and climbing. Why the jump? "We don't have evidence it's because of the Internet," says FTC spokeswoman, Claudia Bourne Farrell, "but everyone thinks it's contributing.[43]"

Another factor is the existence of the hotline that became better known after the director of the FTC's Bureau of Consumer Protection testified before the U.S. Senate in March.

What to Do If It Happens

Whatever the reason for it, you should know what steps to take if your identity gets swiped:

1. Call the police. Make sure you get a copy of any incident report (you may need it for insurance purposes).

2. Call your creditors and the bank that issues your ATM card. Close any affected accounts and get new account numbers (but don't panic, you're not liable for more than $50 in charges you didn't make, and many creditors won't hold you even to that much).

3. Call the fraud lines at the three credit bureaus, and arrange to have a fraud alert put on your account. In that way, someone with your identifying details won't be able to saunter up to the counter at Macy's and open an account in your name.

4. Call the FTC hotline. The commission will put your information into the national data base of identity thieves it is building. This is a very tough crime to control, Farrell notes, "but a trail of information goes a long way."

---

[42] Chatzky, Jean Sherman. *How to Foil Identity Thieves*. New York: Penguin Group, 2007. Print.

[43] Claudia Bourne Farrell, Federal Trade Commission, Bureau of Consumer Protection (statement), 2011.

Fraud at Your Doorstep

These days, it's hard to avoid falling victim to fraud, especially when it comes knocking at your door. Here are some typical scenarios:

1. A dump truck stops in front of a house in a suburban neighborhood, and the driver walks to the door. A seventy-six-year-old woman answers the door and is told by the truck driver that he just came off of a job site and has a load of extra asphalt that he could use on her driveway to make it as good as new. He goes onto to say that it will only cost $500 and she would have a new driveway. She agrees, and pays the man the money. He backs the truck onto her driveway and dumps the contents out. Two hours later, the driver has raked the asphalt out over the driveway and has left. The next morning, she inspects the "new" driveway, and finds that cracks have already started to appear, the surface is not smooth like the old driveway was; the asphalt or tar is wet and sticky in places. Some of it has spilled onto her lawn and flowerbeds, and out into the street.

2. Two men driving a pickup truck with a camper top stop in front of an elderly couple's residence. They tell the couple that they're roofing contractors, and for a small sum of money can do an excellent job sealing their roof from future leaks. The couple agrees and pays money to the men up front. The men are heard working on the roof, but when the husband goes outside an hour later to check on their progress, he finds that they have already left. The men had some buckets of tar and a pair of brooms, and quickly spread the contents out over a portion of the roof and left, never to return.

3. A couple drives up to a house in a cargo van and tells the homeowners that, for a fee, they will clean all the junk out of the attic (they do this with the garage, as well). The two are paid and begin to go to work. While the workers are inside the residence, there is so much distraction that it's difficult for the homeowners to keep track of them. The pair works for an hour or so, and then, while they're both outside at the same time, they get in the van and leave. The

homeowners check the attic and find that some things appear to have been moved around and pushed into a corner, but not a lot has been cleaned up. They just can't locate the few antiques that were stored up there. And, during the next couple of days, they discover that jewelry is missing from their bedroom, and the credit cards can't be found.

Those three scenarios were actual events. There are thousands of scams just like these involving people coming to the door and offering a service for an up-front fee. Sometimes it's a salesman, or salesmen, who just want to get into a house to either commit a robbery or worse, take a look around the house for a future burglary. Perhaps he's just selling some sort of scheme. Whatever the scenario may be, if someone comes to your door unsolicited, do not allow them in and advise them that you're calling the police.

It's relatively easy to spot unlicensed contractors. Here are some things that should tip you off:

> A large down payment is requested before any work begins.

> The full amount is requested before work begins.

> There is a verbal contract only.

> The contractor does not have proof of insurance.

> The homeowner is informed that the job does not require a permit.

> The contractor is only willing to work in the evenings or weekends.

> The contractor displays only an occupational license.

Remember, in most areas a permit is required before a contractor can be hired to perform a job, and a written contract only makes sense. The written contract will outline the work to be done, the total cost for the work and the time expectancy for the job to be completed. In addition to this, a legitimate contractor will never require any money up front, and only expects to be paid in full upon the completion of the job.

As well as an occupational license, the contractor must have current and valid insurance coverage and the paperwork that goes along with it. Legitimate contractors work during the daytime, usually between the hours of 8:00 a.m. to 5:00 p.m., and never on the weekends unless it's with special permission and there are no local ordinances against it.

Other Ways You Can Be Scammed

The following is a list of other types of common frauds and scams, along with a little advice about how to avoid them or what to do about them:

> *Advanced-fee loans:* It is sometimes difficult to obtain a loan if credit ratings are not that good. We normally apply for loans through our banks, credit unions or other financial institutions, and they in turn, in order to protect their investment, must undertake a credit history check before issuing a loan to a borrower. There are some advertisements that suggest a loan can be guaranteed. More often than not, this is called an advanced-fee loan. This is where, for a fee, the company will lock in a loan rate. Remember, loans cannot be guaranteed in advance, no matter whether there is an advanced fee or not. Some legitimate lending institutions do charge you for an application process, and that is not out of the ordinary. If it's an advanced-fee loan, go somewhere else.

> *Art fraud:* A great many pieces of art are actually forgeries or counterfeits. The most popular counterfeit art currently being espoused as the real thing are pieces by Salvador Dali, Pablo Picasso, Marc Chagall and Joan Miro. You may receive a postcard stating that you have won an original art piece. The mailing will be followed by a telephone call. The caller will tell you that due to the high cost of insurance, and shipping and handling for such a piece, it must be paid in advance. Or the caller may try and pressure you into

buying other original or limited-edition art pieces. Just use good common sense here. There are very few original art pieces floating around out there. And if there were, it is doubtful that you or I will be getting a postcard telling us that it's ours for free. The high valued art piece where they're trying to get you to pay the up-front insurance fee is nothing but junk. Any piece of art that you're considering purchasing should be appraised by an independent art appraiser or a museum curator.

➢ *Business opportunities:* You see them advertised everywhere. For someone just starting out in the business world, the advertisements sound very attractive. The advertisements suggest that for working only part-time hours you can potentially earn $80,000 to $100,000 per year. There is an enormous risk to you to even consider one of these ventures. First of all, to actually earn the amount of money they usually suggest would take much more than part-time hours. At the very minimum, you should check their references. But go beyond that, because their references may be what are called "singers," or people who will say all the rights things to make it sound wonderful. If it's a vending machine business, as an example, check the vending companies and the customers whose stores the machines are in. Check with everyone and anyone that remotely has anything to do with the business. Making an informed decision at the very beginning can save you an awful lot of aggravation later on.

➢ *Carpet cleaners:* Some carpet cleaning operations offer promotional advertisements that really do sound too good to be true. They may claim to clean all the first-floor carpets for a certain amount of money. Be careful, there may be some add-on charges. Always get a written estimate from carpet-cleaning companies, and always have someone else with you when the carpet cleaner is in your house. Having a friend by your side ensures that you will not be scammed, that you have a witness to any agreement (making sure that there are no add-on charges) and that the job is done satisfactorily.

➢ *Credit repair scams:* Have you seen the advertisements that say: "Credit problems… no problem" or the one that says, "We can erase your bad credit! 100 percent guaranteed!"? Well, save your money and don't believe them. They all ask for a fee, usually around $50 to $100. And then they may tell you it will take four to six weeks before your credit history has been wiped clean. You will never hear from them again, you will never get your money back and your bad credit history remains. The only thing that has changed is that some of your money is now their money.

There are hundreds of examples of people trying to take your money in some way or another. No matter what the offer, no matter how promising an advertisement may sound, you should always check references, always get a written contract or estimate, never pay any fees or money up front, always call others who may have used those services or products, never believe anyone who comes to your door uninvited or who approaches you on the street, and never believe the advertised promises of unsolicited mail.

Fraud is popular all over the world and, just as an aside, here are a few common examples from the other side of the Atlantic Ocean:

➢ In London and Paris, you can buy opera or theater tickets on the street at a reduced cost. You will find, however, that the tickets are no good, are the cheapest seats in the place, or were for cancelled performances. Always buy those tickets at the box office.

➢ In many European cities, there are mock auctions. These auctions carry no warranties of any kind and the merchandise is usually imitation, cheap and shoddy.

➢ Counterfeit merchandise is for sale on the streets of almost every European city. Use extreme caution when buying anything on the streets. It's always a scam. Computer disks sold on the streets may contain nothing at all, or worse, may contain viruses. The packaging may look real and impressive, but don't be fooled.

➢ 75 percent of counterfeiting in Europe involves computer games.

➢ Beware of short-term leases for flats (apartments) in the United Kingdom. You may be taken to a flat, pay a hefty deposit of around 1,000 pounds and be given a set of keys. The "landlord" will leave, never to be seen again, along with your money. The flat was never his to rent out in the first place.

➢ In England, watch for unlicensed taxi operations; they are illegal. The taxis must be the licensed black taxis that we all know. All others are "touting," are illegal and will often charge you more than they should. Mini-cars are illegal as taxis.

➢ Be very careful of hair stylists in England. Some of them are run out of back shops and the results can be much less than you expect. One woman purchased hair extensions for 700 pounds, and a few days later they all came out. She never got her money back and found out that those hair extensions are usually purchased in bulk and are valued at around 5 pounds.

➢ Clamping of your car's wheel is legal in many European cities, but be careful of all the scams. Someone in hiding will wait for you to park, and when you're out of sight will immediately clamp the wheel. You have to pay at least 75 pounds (in the U.K.) to get the thing off and get your car back.

➢ And in the Philippines, duty-free alcohol is almost always counterfeit. The bottle may look legitimate, but what's inside is watered down.

I could go on and on.

Chapter Thirteen

Automobile Repair Scams

Although this topic is really a continuation of the list of scams in the previous chapter, I thought it deserves its own chapter because the problem of automobile repair scams is so widespread.

Americans spend roughly 90 to 130 billion dollars each year to fix their vehicles, and experts estimate that at least 25 percent to 50 percent of the money is lost to fraud or incompetence[44]. And who are the culprits for all of this? Although the majority of the nation's 810,000 automobile mechanics are honest, there are more than a few bad apples in this barrel. Even the honest mechanics can be goaded by sales incentives that, according to a recent report by the National Association of Attorneys General's Auto Repair Task Force, encourage mechanics to push unnecessary work.

The Top Five Scams

The following are five of the top problems, according to government officials, mechanics, consumer advocates and law enforcement:

1. A small problem is diagnosed as a much bigger one. As an example, most cars built after 1980 have central computers that control many of their systems. When something goes wrong with an electrical switch, for instance, the problem is identified by a sensor, which in turn signals the computer. A mechanic can then locate and replace the faulty switch. That's how it works, in theory. In reality, however, a dishonest mechanic may tell you that the computer itself needs to be replaced. If you fall for this, you will be losing approximately $500 to $1,200. And that money goes to "fix" a nonexistent computer problem.

---

[44] United States. *Operation Broken Trust*. Washington, DC: The National Association of Attorney General's Auto Repair Task Force, 2011. Print.

2. You're charged extra for items that are part of a single repair job. This trick is common with brake repairs. Your mechanic may tell you that you need to recondition your brake drums or rotors (average cost around $160). Your bill, however, doesn't stop at $160 but shows another $95 for repacking the wheel bearings. "They have to do that in order to turn the drum or rotor, and it shouldn't be treated as a separate item," says Maher. "Many consumers don't know that, and wind up paying extra."

3. A low-price deal turns into a big-ticket nightmare. In the state of Florida (of course) in the early 1990s, regulators shut down a chain of repair shops that lured customers with transmission tune-ups for $9.95. Instead of saving $30 or more off the normal cost, customers ended up with large bills for fictitious repairs. "These shops suck you in with an amazing offer and then take your car apart," warns Richard Shedd of California's Bureau of Automotive Repair. "So you're a captive audience when they tell you that's it's a lot worse than they thought.[45]"

4. Car makers pay dealers to fix problems. Why don't we get told this? An estimated 500 hidden warranties are in effect at any one time covering various defects from flaking paint to failing engines. Dealers are usually notified through technical service bulletins from the manufacturer. Only four out of the fifty states require that car owners be notified (California, Connecticut, Virginia and Wisconsin). Double-dipping dealers can charge unknowing customers for repairs that should be free.

5. Needlessly fixing something before it's broken. Overzealous preventive maintenance has become a common scam in the auto repair industry. As an example, you're told that your shock absorbers are fine now, but could "go at any time." It's like somebody telling you to change the light bulbs in your house before they burn out.

---

[45] Richard Shedd, California's Bureau of Auto Report (statement), 2000.

Some old parts, such as radiator hoses and timing belts need to be changed before they fail, but in many cases your car's warning systems (a light indicator on the dash board) will alert you in plenty of time.

What You Can Do to Protect Yourself

Here are some things you can do to keep from falling victim to these scams:

> ➢ Be very skeptical of claims that your entire computer system (or entire anything) needs to be replaced. And for any repairs that seem unusually expensive or extensive, get another opinion. "It's unlikely two mechanics from two garages will try the same rip-off," says Michael Maher, the former Director of the Technical Services Bureau for New York State's Department of Motor Vehicle[46].

> ➢ Your best protection is to get a written estimate of all parts and labor before you commit to anything. That way, if you get a second opinion, you'll be able to directly compare all costs. Be wary of deals that seem too good to be true.

> ➢ While price is a concern, don't focus on that alone. Mechanics, even honest ones, differ widely in their skills. Michigan and Hawaii are the only states that require repair shops to prove they employ only qualified technicians. In the other 48 states it's up to you.

> ➢ Get references from friends, because a personal relationship in these matters is often the best guarantee against scams. Or try to find one of the nearly 5,000 garages approved by the American Automobile Association.

---

[46] Michael P. Maher, former Director of the Technical Services Bureau for New York's State Department of Motor Vehicles (statement), 2004.

➤ Mechanics certified by the National Institute for Automotive Services Excellence are an option. Be aware that a garage with only one ASE certified mechanic can qualify, but that mechanic may be certified in only one of the ASE's eight areas of expertise. Affirm that the mechanic that you use has passed all the appropriate tests for the work you need done.

➤ If you experience car problems that your warranty wouldn't ordinarily cover, ask your dealer if there's a good-will program or a policy adjustment on the problem. "Most dealers are cooperative about such requests, especially if you use the industry lingo," says Clarence Ditlow, the co-author of Little Secrets of the Auto Industry[47]. The National Highway Traffic Safety Administration operates an information hot line at (800) 424-9393 as well as the website www.nhta.dot.gov for consumer access, safety recall information, service bulletins and to register a complaint. You can also write to:

> The Center for Auto Safety
> 2001 South Street NW
> Washington, D.C. 20009

When you write, include the make, model and year of your car, a description of the problem and a self-addressed stamped envelope. You'll receive a current list of service bulletins for your car.

➤ If you have any doubts about a mechanic's diagnosis, get a second opinion. In addition to this, tell the mechanic that you want the worn part after it's replaced. You may not know exactly what you're getting (I usually don't), but just asking for the part may throw off the dishonest mechanic. "Dishonest mechanics don't rip off every customer, only the ones they think are easy to fool," says Allen Wood of California's Bureau of Automotive Repair[48].

---

[47] Ditlow, Clarence. *Little Secrets of the Auto Industry*. Washington, DC: Center for Auto Safety. 1994. Print.

[48] Allen Wood, California's Bureau of Automotive Repair (statement), 2006.

Chapter Fourteen

Automobile Theft

In the United States today, a vehicle is stolen every 17 to 20 seconds, and carjackings occur about 100 times each day. If those statistics make you a little uncomfortable, they should. It is estimated that automobile theft costs Americans around $9 billion per year[49].

What You Need to Know

We all need to be far more vigilant if we are to defeat car thieves. Most are professional criminals who strip older cars and sell the parts for much more money than the actual book value for the car. They are less often teenagers out for a joy ride in a hot, new car, like they used to be years ago.

The most frequently stolen vehicles are eight or nine years old with low book value. The most frequently stolen newer vehicles are utility and sports vehicles, as well as luxury cars, while station wagons and passenger vans are less frequently stolen.

According to a study conducted by the National Insurance Crime Bureau, your vehicle is more likely to be stolen if you live in a coastal or border community[50]. Every year car thieves steal hundreds of thousands of American vehicles, and ship them overseas or drive them across U.S. borders.

Criminals are increasingly turning to an even more desperate form of automobile theft, known as carjacking, in which a vehicle is forcibly taken from a motorist. Carjackers may stage events such as a minor rear-end collision, often at stoplights or stop signs. If you get out to inspect your car you will be robbed, usually battered, and your car will be stolen.

---

[49] Ditlow, Clarence. *Automobile Theft*. Washington, DC: the Center for Auto Safety, 2009. Print.

[50] Schmidt, Brian. *Theft and Fraud Awareness*. Washington, DC: the National Insurance Crime Bureau, 2008. Print.

What You Can Do

You can protect yourself from car thieves with the following basic precautions:

> ➢ Consider having your vehicle's windows etched with the vehicle's identification number (VIN).

> ➢ File the automobile's title in your home or office, and carry the registration in your wallet.

> ➢ Keep the house and car keys on separate key rings without identifying tags.

> ➢ Consider equipping your car with a cell phone (or carry one on you), Citizen's Band radio (CB) or anti-theft deterrent. Check the vehicle theft prevention checkup booklet to determine which device is best for your car. You may want to consider a LoJack device for your car.

> ➢ Enroll in a reliable emergency road service.

> ➢ Never leave the car running in your driveway or while you dash into a convenience store.

> ➢ Always take your keys with you.

> ➢ Always close and lock the windows, doors and sunroof. Four out of five cars stolen were left unlocked by the owners. Remember — thieves are opportunists. Just don't give them any opportunities.

> ➢ When parking, choose a spot in a populated, well-lit area.

> ➢ Don't park next to a van, truck, dumpster or anywhere thieves could be hiding.

> ➢ Park with the front wheels turned sharply to the curb and apply the emergency brake to prevent thieves from towing your car.

➢ When parking in an attended lot, choose a spot close to the attendant's station, and if you are using valet parking, leave only the ignition key with the valet.

➢ Choose an open, rather than closed, garage for greater visibility. If possible, park on the ground level to avoid using the elevators and stairways.

➢ When returning to your vehicle, remember those safety precautions I mentioned earlier and have your keys ready. Check the interior of the car for any intruders and look all around you.

Here are some bits of advice to keep you from becoming a carjacking victim:

➢ Be an alert driver. Pay attention to what's happening around you.

➢ Don't apply makeup or read at stoplights.

➢ Don't talk on your cell phone when driving, unless in an emergency. Do not text while driving or while parked anywhere. Keep your car in motion where possible.

➢ Never stay in your parked car eating, reading or sleeping.

➢ Know that 77 percent of carjacking thieves are armed.

➢ Be prepared, because most carjackings happen so quickly, around 12 to 15 seconds, that victims usually don't have time to think through their reactions.

➢ Know also that most carjackings occur at night, and nearly half happen on Fridays, Saturdays and Sundays, and usually in urban areas.

➢ Check the rearview mirror often to make sure that you're not being followed into your driveway or garage.

➤ If you suspect that you are being targeted for a carjacking, keep driving and try to find a populated, well-lighted area, or a police or fire department. Call the police from your cell phone immediately. (You do carry a cell phone, right?)

➤ Remember the previous warnings about things such as infant seats on the roadway or eggs thrown at your windshield. Anything weird or unusual usually means trouble.

➤ Lost or confused drivers are vulnerable. Know where you're going and how to get there. Call ahead for safe directions.

➤ Drive with all doors locked. Leave the windows rolled up. If it's hot, use the air conditioner.

➤ When pulling up behind another car at a stoplight, leave enough space in front of you for a quick emergency escape.

➤ Keep all personal belongings, including handbags, briefcases and packages, under the seats or on the floor out of sight.

➤ Make a mental note of those police and fire station locations.

➤ If approached by strangers, drive away quickly (if possible). Never get out of your car, unlock the doors or roll down your windows for strangers—ever. If you have to, blow the horn for attention, and don't stop blowing the thing until help arrives or the danger has passed.

If you end up being the victim of a carjacking, don't feel as if you have to reach for your purse or other valuables. Those are just material things and can be replaced. You, on the other hand, are irreplaceable. Leave everything behind and get away.

Theft Prevention Scorecard

The National Insurance Crime Bureau (NICB) has developed a theft-prevention checkup list. The checkup includes the following questionnaire to help you determine how many layers of protection you need for your vehicle:

Location:

What is your city's population?
More than 250,000 = 8 points
250,000 to 100,001 = 6 points
100,000 to 50,001 = 4 points
50,000 to 10,000 = 2 points
Less than 10,000 = 0 points
Although the trend is changing, the Federal Bureau of Investigation's data indicates that city drivers are still more likely to become the victims of vehicle theft than suburban motorists.

Automobile Style:

What type of vehicle do you drive?
Sports car = 5 points
Luxury car = 4 points
Utility vehicle = 4 points
Sedan = 3 points
Passenger van = 1 point
Station wagon = 0 points
According to the Highway Loss Data Institute, the style of your vehicle is one of the biggest factors in determining its theft rate.[51]

Age:

How old is your vehicle?
0 to 5 years = 2 points
6 to 9 years = 1 point
10 + years = 0 points

---

[51] Rader, Russ. *HLDI Consumer Brochure*. Arlington, VA: the Highway Loss Data Institute, 2009. Print.

According to the NICB, middle-aged vehicles are actually stolen more often than newer vehicles. Stolen vehicle parts often become replacement parts for other aging vehicles.

Bonus:

Add one point to your score if you live near an international border or port. According to an NICB study, and law enforcement documentation, vehicle theft rates in coastal and border communities are higher than the national average. Vehicles stolen in these communities are often shipped or driven to foreign countries.

Total your points from the preceding four categories:

Location =
Style =
Age =
Bonus =
Total =

What the Scores Mean

The higher the points for your vehicle, the higher the risk of it being stolen. The higher the risk, the more layers of protection you will need. The following four layers of protection are recommended by law enforcement sources and the NICB:

0 to 6 points=Use common sense.
> Securing your vehicle and parking in well-lit areas are the simplest and most effective ways to thwart would-be car thieves.

7 to 10 points=Consider using warning devices.
> A device which alerts thieves that your vehicle is protected before they attempt to steal it can also protect your vehicle from burglary and vandalism.

11 to 13 points=Consider adding immobilizing devices.

These devices prevent thieves from bypassing your ignition and hotwiring the vehicle: They include electronic keys, kill switches and fuse cut-offs.

14 to 16 points=For added protection, use tracking devices. This final layer of protection is a tracking system, such as LoJack, which emits a signal to police when the vehicle is reported as stolen. The signal can lead law enforcement authorities right to your car.

Chapter Fifteen

Road Rage

According to law enforcement statistics and a report published by *Car and Travel* magazine, if you think life on the road has gotten nastier and more brutish of late, you're not alone[52]. A study sponsored by the American Automobile Association Foundation for Traffic Safety confirms what many drivers already suspect: aggressive driving has progressively increased during this last decade[53]. "From 1992 to 2012 the incidences of road rage have increased dramatically," says J. Talbot Barns, an international traffic safety advisor. "What was an isolated case in 1990, is now taken for granted.[54]"

The study analyzed more than 10,000 police reports and newspaper stories about traffic incidents that led to violence. It found that reports of violent traffic incidents have increased nearly 7 percent since 1990. Those figures are now up another 5 percent. "This is only the small tip of a very large iceberg," says David K. Willis, president of the AAA Foundation for Traffic Safety. "For every aggressive driving incident serious enough to result in a police report or newspaper article, there are hundreds or thousands more that never get reported to the authorities.[55]"

Barns indicates that it is now unusual to go for a drive and not be involved in or see an incident of rude behavior on the part of another driver, or even actual road rage. In the reports studied, a total of 12,610 people were injured and 218 killed as the result of aggressive driving.

The AAA study also found that events precipitating violent incidents are often remarkably trivial, including slow driving, failing to use a turn signal or cutting off another driver. "People have been shot because they drove too slowly or played the radio too loudly," Willis says.

---

[52] Hoffman, Carl. "Wish You Weren't Here." *Car and Travel*, 2009. Print.

[53] Ronis, Carol. *2010 Traffic Safety Culture Index*: the AAA Foundation for Traffic Safety, 2010. Print.

[54] J. Talbot Barnes, international traffic safety advisor (statement), 2012.

[55] David K. Willis, AAA Foundation for Traffic Safety (statement), 1996.

Preliminary reports from a study now under way by the AAA indicates that one-fifth, 20 percent, of all injury-related crashes may have a road-rage connection. That study, being conducted in twelve states from coast to coast, is due out in 2013, but the preliminary statistics are horrifying.

And just who are the aggressive drivers? According to the AAA study, it can be just about anyone. Although the majority of the aggressive drivers studied were males between the ages of eighteen and twenty-six, drivers as old as seventy-five were reported as having driven aggressively. And though most aggressors had criminal records, histories of violence or drug or alcohol problems, hundreds of others were successful people with no such histories.

Barns believes that subtle changes have crept into the American psyche, beginning in the early 1990s. He says, "From the top to the bottom, from the White House to the local janitor, people just think they can get away with anything, and that being courteous and kind are now passé. Those changes may become less transparent when we get behind the wheel of a car."

The car itself was the weapon of choice for 23 percent of aggressive drivers, while firearms, knives, clubs or tire irons were used in 44 percent of the incidents. Pepper spray, golf clubs, eggs and even a crossbow have been used against fellow motorists and law enforcement officers by aggressive drivers.

Tips for Avoiding Road Rage

The following are a few suggestions that may keep you out of harm's way:

➢ Never make obscene gestures.

➢ Use your horn sparingly.

➢ Don't tailgate.

➢ Don't block the passing lane. Even if you're going the speed limit and not one mile over it, move over. If you're being tailgated, move over.

➢ Never take more than one parking space. Parking disputes

frequently escalate. Also, never use a disabled space if you're not disabled. Besides being discourteous and illegal, it is a frequent flashpoint for disputes with other motorists.

➢ Never stop your car in the middle of the road to talk to a pedestrian or other driver.

➢ Don't inflict loud music on neighboring cars.

➢ Don't switch lanes without using your directional signal; it's illegal and dangerous.

➢ Don't use your high-beam headlights unnecessarily.

➢ Don't take traffic problems personally.

➢ Avoid eye contact with an aggressive driver.

➢ Stay cool and don't react to provocation.

➢ Keep away from drivers behaving erratically.

➢ Above all, never underestimate the other driver's capacity for mayhem.

Chapter Sixteen

Safety at the ATM

If you use an ATM machine, you stand a very good chance of being robbed, depending on where, when, and how you use it. The reason for this is that many ATMs are used at night, and a great many have to be accessed after you exit your automobile. If they're used at night, it means that the bank, and probably the surrounding businesses are closed. It also means that it might be dark in the area. You're also accessing your bank account and receiving money. It's the perfect breeding ground for criminals.

When using an ATM, take into account all of the advice that's been given throughout this book, and also use these precautions:

➢ Prepare for your transaction at home (such as filling out a deposit slip) to minimize your time at the ATM or night-deposit facility.

➢ Mark each transaction in your account record, but not while at the ATM.

➢ Always save your ATM receipts. Don't leave them (or any other documents) at the ATM, because they may contain important account information.

➢ Compare your records with the account statements you receive.

➢ Don't lend your ATM card to anyone.

➢ Make sure you don't forget your card when you leave the ATM.

➢ Protect the secrecy of your Personal Identification Number (PIN). Don't reveal it to anyone, and don't write it where it can be discovered, such as in your wallet or your purse.

➢ Prevent others from seeing you enter your PIN by using your body to shield their view.

➤ If you lose your ATM card or if it's stolen, call the police right away, and contact your bank as soon as possible. You should consult the other disclosures you have received about electronic fund transfers for additional information about what to do if your card is lost or stolen.

➤ When you make a transaction, be aware of your surroundings. Look out for suspicious activity near the ATM or night deposit facility, particularly if it is after sunset.

➤ At night, be sure that the facility (including the parking area and walkways) is well-lit. Consider having someone accompany you when you use the facility at night.

➤ If you observe any problems at the ATM, do not exit your vehicle, but instead drive to another ATM. Call the police immediately.

➤ Don't accept assistance from anyone you don't know when using an ATM.

➤ If you notice anything suspicious, or if any other problem arises after you have begun an ATM transaction, you may want to cancel the transaction, pocket your card and leave. Be very cautious. Call the police. Find another ATM or come back later.

➤ Don't display your cash. Pocket it as soon as the ATM transaction is completed and count it later when you are in the safety of your home or other secure area.

➤ At a drive-up ATM facility, make sure that your car doors are locked and all of the windows are rolled up (except, of course, the driver's window). Keep the engine running, the transmission in drive (not in park) and remain alert to your surroundings.

➢ If you see anything at all out of the ordinary as you drive up to one of these facilities, do not exit your car. Keep driving and call the police as soon as possible.

➢ If you notice any lights out at the facility, or any damage, let the bank know as soon as possible so that they can take care of the situation.

Chapter Seventeen

Dating Services

Beware of dating services that offer you the answer to your dreams. A great many of these agencies are little more than back-room operations that feed on the dreams and vulnerabilities of others. Some figures suggest that a full two-thirds of all the dating services in this country are little more than licenses to steal. The following case, in which I was asked to assist the Dade County Police in Miami, illustrates what can happen:

A divorced woman, mother of two small children, contacted one of these services and was told that for $2,000 her name and information would be placed in a database. The database would match her personality, education, lifestyle and interests with the man of her dreams. She could ill afford the money, but decided to take out an unsecured bank loan. The money was then paid to the service, and within two weeks she received three possible matches.

Of the three men she was somewhat interested in, she chose the one she thought most closely matched her in every way. He was a widower and a father who owned a lucrative business. She contacted him and arranged a date for the following week. The date went quite well, and over the course of the next few weeks she entered into a relationship with the man. He moved into her apartment, even though she had yet to see his home. She was somewhat suspicious, but was now in love. She even trusted the guy with her children and allowed him to pick them up at the day-care facility.

After a little more than a week of this, she arrived home after work, but the man of her dreams was gone, and so were her two children. The few pieces of jewelry given to her by her grandmother were missing and her bank account had been cleaned out. The subsequent investigation revealed that the man was actually a convicted rapist and suspected pedophile and was wanted in three states. As of now, the children are still missing, and he has yet to be caught.

While this may not be the typical outcome of using a dating service, it does point to a very real danger. The dating service that the woman used had told her that they screen all of the people who apply. What they meant by this is that they conduct background checks on their clients, but there was most certainly not a background check done on this man. Most dating services do not even bother with any sort of background checks whatsoever. Dating services are simply there to take your money. They don't care about anything else.

Background checks are cost-prohibitive, and these agencies will not spend the money to thoroughly check any of their clientele. There may indeed be an exception or two, but I have never seen it. Criminal history checks are not conducted because they are normally only available to law-enforcement agencies and, even if they were available, people would be screaming about their rights to privacy. And I wouldn't blame them.

General Precautions

I could actually walk into a dating service, tell them that my name was Count Lazslow I'llscamski, and say that I'm an extremely wealthy widower with financial holdings in five countries. And that is exactly what would appear in my database. They couldn't possibly do a check on me because they would have to go through Interpol for the international connection, and Interpol would laugh them off the telephone. And it wouldn't matter if I were Charles Manson, the Son of Sam or the late Osama bin Laden. They would not know. I could be wanted for rape and murder; I could be a drug addict or infected with the AIDS virus, and they would have no idea. Neither would you, until it's too late.

There are literally hundreds of cases of rapes, sexual assaults, child molestations, theft and assault–and–battery perpetrated by people using dating services to win the trust of their victims. Most of the cases are not as horrendous as the one I described, but they are all very serious and the instances of criminal acts are steadily growing.

States are more or less powerless to enforce any sort of control over dating services, but there may be some legislation on the horizon which, if enacted into law, would place some limitations on these moneymaking entities. In the meantime what are some steps that we can take to avoid the pitfalls associated with dating services? The most obvious solution is to not use them in the first place. Bars and clubs are referred to as "meat markets," yet there must be a sensible alternative. But you must be cautious about this, and if you do decide to use a dating service, check them out beforehand.

One way to do this is to contact the Better Business Bureau. If there have been previous complaints or concerns voiced about a particular service, they may have the information on file. If there is something on file, do not use the service. Don't, however, let the Better Business Bureau be the deciding factor in your decision-making. They may not have all the details about an entity. Remember, all you have to do is pay a fee to be listed with them.

It would be better to contact the law-enforcement agency in your area to see if there are any investigations being conducted against a service. They can't give you too many details about an ongoing investigation, but they can tell you that there *is* an investigation. They may also be able to tell you about previous investigations. Most of the information is public knowledge and should be available for you. If there are any ongoing or previous investigations, don't use the service.

A third way to check out a dating service is to check with the Attorney General's Office or State Attorney's Office in your area. Here are some other things you can do:

> ➤ Before you enter into a contractual relationship with a dating service, ask for several names and telephone numbers of previous clients with whom you could speak regarding their experiences with the company. If you get any negative responses, do not use the service. If the service cannot or will not provide a list of references, go elsewhere.

> ➤ Ask to meet with the management of the service and request a tour of the facility. If those requests are denied, do not use the service. Many services have a post office box for an address. If there is only a post office box number and not an actual physical address, go elsewhere. If, on the other hand, there is indeed an address, you might consider driving by the location before you contact them. Most of these operations are not located in garden spots, but instead are back-room, here-today-and-gone-tomorrow types of entities. Be very cautious and careful.

In dealing with dating services, remember the rule about not allowing anyone access or control of you, your family or your property. You must use your instincts and good common sense.

International Agencies

And now, just a few words about those international agencies that offer you the excitement of meeting women from Europe, Asia and South America. These are usually directed at men. Guys, if you haven't believed anything I've written in this book thus far, please believe me now. Unless you're willing to throw your money away, you must avoid those dating/introduction agencies. If you think that money is tight right here in the United States when it comes to conducting background checks, wait until you deal with the foreign companies. These agencies have turned into a multimillion dollar enterprise on a number of continents. And some are actually foreign companies operating in the United States. Once your money goes into their coffers, what possible motivation would they have to produce what they advertise? The banks are, for the most part, located overseas, and trying to obtain reimbursements from the agencies is just about impossible.

Some of the advertisements from these agencies sound awfully enticing. Here are a few recent ones:

"10,000+ BEAUTIFUL LATIN SINGLES (or beautiful Russian singles) seek........"

"Asian Beauties, affectionate and loving"

"Come on, men, let's get those hormones under control. You really don't have to look very far; there are plenty of absolutely gorgeous and highly intelligent women right here in the United States."

The advertisements can make you believe that the woman you're looking for is just a telephone call away. The reality is, however, that it will cost you several thousand dollars just to get to the point where introductions are made (if you ever get that far). And it may well turn out that the beautiful woman on all of those photographs you received is not the woman you're now talking to. And by the way, those very same photographs are in the hands of several hundred other American men who believed, like you, that the beautiful woman in the photograph could be their future wife.

The services that do actually have some women willing to meet American men have not conducted any sort of background investigation whatsoever. And in many cases the services may have actually fabricated most of the information they make available for you. You may be told wonderful things about a person, but the reality is probably something else entirely.

According to Phillip Moureau of Interpol, "We have so little control of these agencies, and they are free to advertise in most magazines and newspapers in the United States and here in Europe.[56]" Please be careful when you consider trying to contact them. As an aside, you should know that Interpol has a number of ongoing investigations related to international dating services, and more than one Russian agency has been directly linked to the Russian mafia.

---

[56] Phillip Moureau, Interpol (statement), 2009.

Chapter Eighteen

Illegal Drugs — What You Need to Know

Illegal drugs have, unfortunately, become a part of our lives here in the United States and elsewhere. There are a number of them in circulation, but there are some that are particularly dangerous and are having a significant impact on our society and culture.

Methamphetamine

One of the most insidious and relatively new drugs being used today: is methamphetamine, known on the streets by various names, including "crank," "speed," "ice," "meth" as well as a few others. It comes in a variety of colors but usually is a yellowish rock-like chunk, or is in a crystal powder form. It can be smoked, injected (this is known as "slamming"), ingested or snorted (inhaled into nasal passages).

The effects from this drug are dramatic, and some studies suggest that it has become as popular as cocaine. One such study conducted in 1997 indicated that methamphetamine users age twelve and older had reached 5.3 million in the United States[57]. The last figure I heard about was closer to 7.7 million. The death rate for this drug has tripled in the last ten years.

This is how the drug works: It goes deep inside the brain where neurotransmitters (natural biochemicals) shuttle between gaps in the neurons. Dopamine is the neurotransmitter most associated with pleasure. Too little of this can result in depression, while too much can create the frenzied actions associated with a manic state. A moderately heightened level, however, produces good feelings and euphoria. Dopamine levels are usually held in check by a molecular mechanism that effectively stores the excess for future use. Methamphetamine, as well as cocaine, keeps the dopamine in circulation, allowing feelings of euphoria to last. But methamphetamine, unlike cocaine, goes well beyond this and directly stimulates the brain cells to release even more dopamine. As use of this drug continues, the brain decreases the production of neurotransmitters. The result is that it soon takes ever-

---

[57] Unknown Author(s). *1997 Newsletter*. Hollywood: Narconon, 1997. Print.

increasing amounts of the drug to achieve the same high, or feelings of euphoria, and the drug user quickly begins to engage in compulsive behavior.

There are a number of physical indicators that we can use to easily spot someone who may be using methamphetamine, as well as a few other kinds of drugs:

> Rapid weight loss.

> Excessive sweating, especially above the upper lip and around the eyebrows.

> Methamphetamine raises blood pressure which in turn constricts blood vessels in the face. This produces a pale, sickly looking countenance.

There are also behavioral changes associated with the use of methamphetamine, among them:

> Hyperactivity

> Euphoria

> Rapid and confusing speech

> Irritability

> Aggressiveness

> Being argumentative

> Sleeplessness

> Lack of interest regarding personal hygiene

> Lost interest in friends and activities, or studies

> Feelings of paranoia

> Compulsive and/or repetitive behavior

Any one, or any combination, of the above behavioral changes may indicate the use of drugs. If you suspect that someone you know, perhaps even your child, is using drugs, you should seek help and guidance immediately. Absolutely do not put this off for a moment.

Methamphetamine not only addicts children and teenagers; it has also become popular with adults. Many people love this drug because it offers quick weight loss, and it gives the feelings of having escaped reality. People who are troubled because of work, difficult finances or unhealthy/unsatisfying relationships turn to this drug. It offers an almost instant escape from their problems. But of course, once initiated into the use of the drug, the user is quickly addicted. And addiction to this drug can and often does lead to death.

Rohypnol, the 'Date Rape' Drug

I recently learned about a case in Providence, Rhode Island, where a young woman reported waking up naked in a fraternity house. She told the investigating officers that she woke up and found herself in unfamiliar surroundings with unfamiliar people. She told them that she may have been sexually assaulted, but was not sure. The only thing she remembered is drinking with a group of people at a local bar. Subsequent tests conducted at Rhode Island Hospital confirmed that she had been raped and may have been under the influence of Rohypnol. On the same day this took place, 527 similar cases were reported in cities and towns across the United States.

Rohypnol is a brand name for flunitrazepam (a benzodiazepine), a very potent tranquilizer similar in nature to valium (diazepam) but much stronger. This drug produces a sedative effect, amnesia, muscle relaxation and a slowing of psychomotor responses. Sedation usually occurs 20 to 30 minutes after the administration of the drug, and can last for several hours.

The drug is often distributed on the street in its original bubble packaging, which adds an air of legitimacy and makes it appear to be legal. This particular drug is not commonly used by physicians in the United States and is not even listed in the *Physician's Desk Reference*.

Use of this drug was initially reported in Florida and Texas, but has now become now widespread. It is known by various street names such as "roachies," "la roache," "rope," "roofies," "ruffies," "rophies" and "rump," in Australia is known as "stupefi." You may have heard it referred to as the "date rape drug." Some rapists frequent bars and buy women drinks, which they lace with the pill by opening a capsule and spilling the contents into the drink. It dissolves quickly, is invisible, tasteless and odorless. All they need to do then is to wait the 20 to 30 minutes.

The drug is also named the "forget pill" because most victims report that they wake up without any memory of being assaulted, and have only a vague memory of who they may have been with at the bar the night before. Rohypnol is considered by many to be the Quaalude — or recreational drug of choice — of the new millennium.

Taken alone this flunitrazepam, like other benzodiazepines, is unlikely to cause death. Taken with alcohol, however, the likelihood of death is increased, due to enhanced central nervous system depression. Rohypnol intoxication is generally associated with impaired judgment as well as impaired motor skills.

According to Gary Ludwig, the chief paramedic and Emergency Services Bureau chief for the St. Louis Fire Department in Missouri, the dangers don't stop there. He says:

"Besides the worries of unprotected sex and the dangerous practice of mixing Rohypnol with alcohol or other drugs, it can lead to dependence when taken repeatedly. An amnesia-producing effect of 'roofies' may prevent users from remembering how or why they took the drug or even that they were given it by others. This makes investigation of sexually related or other offenses very difficult and may account for repeated reports of date rapes involving the use of the drug.[58]"

This drug is now the "in" drug on high school and college campuses throughout the country, and is available for the low cost of $2 to $4 per tablet in most locations. The drug is being used in combination with alcohol and/or heroin, with the idea of intensifying the high of heroin or the buzz of alcohol, or even as a parachute to come down from a cocaine high.

Club Drugs

"Club drugs" are increasingly being used by young adults at all-night dance parties such as "raves" or "trances," dance clubs and bars. MDMA (ecstasy), GHB, Rohypnol, ketamine, methamphetamine

---

[58] Gary Ludwig, "D.C. EMS Worker's Procedures Questioned". *Firehouse Magazine*. 2010.

and LSD are some of the club or party drugs gaining in popularity. Recent studies have shown that the use of club drugs can cause serious long-term health problems, and in many cases death.

If your child is considering attending a "rave" or "trance," please understand what he or she will encounter. At all of these gatherings there are mixed bags (my expression) of drugs made available in vast quantities, and everyone (including your teenager or young adult) is expected to indulge. Peer pressure and the use of alcohol break down any inhibitions, and they are pushed into using these drugs. Do not think for one moment that it won't happen, because it most certainly will. Here are some of the drugs commonly in use at these parties:

Ecstasy

Ecstasy is a derivative of amphetamine. Its chemical name is 3,4 methylenedioxy-N-methylamphetamine (MDMA), and it has a similar structure to methamphetamine. It goes by the street names of "X," "XTC," "Adam," "M&M," "E" and many others. Unlike cocaine, morphine or even nicotine, ecstasy is synthesized in clandestine laboratories (along with several other so-called designer drugs) by altering the structure of the amphetamine molecule. Since it is synthesized in laboratories, its purity can vary substantially from lab to lab, and other compounds are easily combined into the same tablet. Contaminants often include caffeine, ephedrine, ketamine (a hallucinogen) and methamphetamine.

Ecstasy affects the user within just a few minutes of ingestion. The short-term effects of this drug are the altered effects of cognition (thinking), mood, and memory. In other words, ecstasy alters brain chemistry. Short-term (acute) effects include elevated mood and feelings of empathy. The drug is also reinforcing, meaning that its pleasurable properties increase the likelihood that the person will take it again and again (good news for the drug pushers) until death.

People obviously take the drug for its pleasurable or reinforcing effects. Drugs that produce those effects, however, also come with considerable side effects. These include negative psychological effects such as clouded thinking, agitation and disturbed behavior. Other adverse effects include sweating, dry mouth (thirst), increased heart rate, fatigue, muscle spasms (especially jaw-clenching) and hypothermia. It disrupts the ability of the body to regulate temperature.

Some people take multiple doses of the drug in one night. This is sometimes referred to as "stacking." Repeated doses, however, can often cause death. Heart injury due to hypothermia, hypertension (high blood pressure), cardiac arrhythmias (irregular heart beat), muscle breakdown and renal failure due to salt and fluid depletion are a few of the causes of death.

Long-term detrimental effects may be devastating. Some studies suggest that ecstasy users may suffer from verbal and visual memory impairment. And the ability to think or to reason might be permanently altered. Studies are also suggesting a link with the drug to the increased likelihood of kidney disease and kidney failure as well as the early onset of Parkinson's Disease.

GHB

GHB is the abbreviation for Gamma-hydroxbutyrate. It is really a liquid form of ecstasy and is known on the streets by various names including "G," "LX," "LQ," "liquid ecstasy," "Georgia Home Boy," as well as other assorted names. The sedative effects of GHB can result in deep sleep, coma and death.

Ketamine

Ketamine, called "K" or "Special K" is an anesthetic. Use of only a small amount of ketamine results in loss of attention span, learning ability and memory. At higher doses it will cause delirium, amnesia, high blood pressure, depression, severe breathing problems or death.

LSD

LSD, short for Lysergic Acid Diethylamide, is known by various street names including "acid," "LD," "drops," "hit," "sock," etc. It causes unpredictable behavior, depending on the amount taken. Feelings of numbness, weakness, nausea, increased heart rate, sweating, lack of appetite and sleeplessness are not unusual. Using the drug just one time can cause flashbacks many years later.

Cocaine

Cocaine, it is a powerful central nervous system stimulant that heightens alertness, inhibits appetite and the need for sleep, and provides intense feelings of pleasure. It is prepared from the leaf of the erythoxlyon coca bush, which grows primarily in Colombia and Peru.

The initial resurgence of cocaine in the 1960s was largely confined to the affluent, due to its high cost[59]. Part of the drug's mystique was its association with celebrities in the music and sports industries and world of show business. Today, people from all walks of life use it. Young single males are the most frequent users, and there is no clear connection between its use and educational level, occupation or socioeconomic status.

In 1997, approximately 1.5 million Americans ages twelve and older were chronic cocaine users. That figure was a substantial drop from the 1985 statistic of 5.7 million American users. Now, however, there appears to be yet another resurgence in its use, and this year's figures are gradually approaching the 6 million mark.

Cocaine is generally sold on the streets as a hydrochloride salt, which is a fine, white crystalline powder known as "coke," "C," "snow," "flake" or "blow." Street dealers dilute it with inert (nonpsychoactive) but similar-looking substances such as cornstarch, talcum powder and sugar, or with active drugs such as procaine or benzocaine (used as local anesthetics), or with other CNS stimulants such as amphetamines. Illicit cocaine has actually become purer over the years, according to the Royal Canadian Mounted Police (RCMP), and from 1998 to today its purity averages around 75 percent[60].

Cocaine in powder form is usually snorted into the nostrils, although it also may be rubbed onto the mucous lining of the mouth, rectum or vagina. To experience cocaine's effects more quickly, and to heighten its intensity, users sometimes inject it.

Cocaine hydrochloride can be chemically altered to remove other substances. The process, called "freebasing," is potentially dangerous because the solvents used are highly flammable. The pure form of cocaine that results ("free base") is smoked, rather than snorted. The drug commonly called "crack" is a crude form of free

---

[59] Unknown Author(s). *Annual Report – 2010. Washington, DC*: the National Drug Enforcement Administration, 2010. Print.

[60] *Report of the Illicit Drug Situation in Canada*. Ottawa: Prepared by the National Intelligence Analysis, Criminal Intelligence Division, Royal Canadian Mounted Police, 2007. Print.

base.

Cocaine's short-term effects appear soon after a single dose and disappear within a few minutes or hours. Taken in small amounts (up to 100 milligrams), cocaine usually makes the user feel euphoric, energetic, talkative and mentally alert, especially to the sensations of sight, sound and touch. It can also temporarily dispel the need for food and sleep. Paradoxically, it can make some people feel contemplative, anxious or even panic-stricken. Some people find that the drug helps them perform simple physical and intellectual tasks more quickly, while others experience just the opposite effect.

Physical symptoms of cocaine use include accelerated heartbeat and breathing, elevated blood pressure and increased body temperature. Larger amounts (several hundred milligrams or more) intensify the user's high, but may also lead to bizarre, erratic and violent behavior. These users may experience tremors, vertigo, muscle twitches and spasms, a numbing of the throat muscles, paranoia or a toxic reaction closely resembling amphetamine poisoning. Other symptoms include chest pains, nausea, blurred vision, fever, muscle spasms, convulsions, coma and death. Death can result from the convulsions, heart failure or the depression of vital brain centers controlling respiration.

Users also suffer mood swings, loss of interest in sex, weight loss, and insomnia. Chronic cocaine snorting often causes stuffiness, runny nose, eczema around the nostrils and a perforated nasal septum. Users who inject the drug risk not only overdosing, but also infections from nonsterile needles and hepatitis or AIDS. Severe respiratory tract irritation has been noted in heavy users of cocaine free base.

Drug dependence is both physiological and psychological. It affects the user's perceptions of life. With the repeated administration over time, users experience the drug's long-term effects. Euphoria is gradually displaced by restlessness, extreme excitability, insomnia and paranoia, and eventually hallucinations and delusions. Increasingly in need of the drug, the user is in a downward spiral. Early detection and intervention/treatment are critical if the user is to survive. These conditions, clinically identical to amphetamine psychosis and very similar to paranoid schizophrenia, can disappear in some cases after cocaine use is ended.

Heroin

According to the U.S. Drug Enforcement Administration (DEA), "The use of heroin, a narcotic derivative of the opium poppy plant, poses a grave danger to the United States." The DEA considers heroin a serious threat due to its expanded availability, cheap price and increasing abuse, as well as the devastating social and health consequences of heroin addiction.

Pure heroin is a white powder with an extremely bitter taste. Most illicit heroin is distributed in powder form and may vary in color from white to dark brown because of impurities left over from the manufacturing process or the presence of additives. During the last decade, the purity of street heroin went up from 1 percent to 10 percent, to approximately 98 percent. And that is especially so of the heroin smuggled in from South America. The national purity average is right around 41 percent.

Heroin is most often injected, but high-purity heroin may also be snorted or smoked.

Another form of heroin is known as "black tar." This is produced primarily in Mexico. It may be sticky (much like roofing tar) or hard (sort of like coal). Its color ranges from dark brown to black. The color and consistency of black tar heroin results from the crude processing methods used to illicitly manufacture heroin in Mexico. Black tar heroin is most often sold on the streets in its tar-like state with purities ranging from 20 percent to 80 percent. It is most frequently dissolved, diluted and then injected.

The effects that heroin has on users include euphoria, drowsiness, respiratory depression, constricted pupils and nausea. Effects of heroin overdose include slow and shallow breathing, clammy skin, convulsions, coma and death.

According to the Drug Abuse Warning Network, which tracks drug-abuse deaths and emergency room episodes in most major cities in the United States, there was a steady increase in the number of heroin-related deaths from 1992 to 1998. And those numbers are still steadily increasing[61].

During the Clinton administration, a blind eye was turned to the ominous threat of dangerous drugs, including heroin, coming into the United States. During that period of time, the message was clearly

---

[61] Substance Abuse and Mental Health Services Administration. *Annual Report*. Rockwell, MD: the Drug Abuse Warning Network, 2000. Print.

given that the United States was not interested in the proactive enforcement of the crime or the prosecution of the criminals. Too little was done too late, and the consequences to our society, and to the world's population, is only just now beginning to be understood.

Heroin is smuggled into the United States from major manufacturing and distribution centers in Southwest Asia (Iran, Afghanistan, Pakistan and Turkey), Southeast Asia (the Golden Triangle areas of Thailand, Laos and Myanmar), South America (predominately Colombia and Peru), as well as Mexico, Nigeria and West Africa. (By the way, since you've seen Nigeria named more than once in this book, you can safely conclude that it has become somewhat of a hotbed of crime and criminal enterprise.)

Marijuana

Marijuana has been used as an agent for achieving euphoria since ancient times. It was described in a Chinese medical compendium dating all the way back to around 2737 B.C. Its use spread to India and to North Africa, and then to Europe around 500 A.D. It was brought to this country by the Spanish in 1545.

Mexico had become a significant exporter of the drug, but in 1975 the Mexican government agreed to eradicate the crops by spraying them with the herbicide Paraquat. Mexico, however, is undergoing an enormous resurgence in the drug-trade business, with violence at all-time highs and with illicit drugs flowing north across our porous southern borders. Colombia is also a major player in the drug scene, and many of the drugs earmarked for the United States now come across-country through Mexico.

The zero-tolerance climate of the Reagan and Bush administrations resulted in the passage of strict laws and mandatory sentences for drug trafficking. During the subsequent Clinton/Gore administration, however, there was an obvious relaxation of the enforcement efforts. And, according to the international drug rehabilitation program Narconon, the result was "after over a decade of decreased use, marijuana-smoking began an upward trend, especially among teenagers."

Marijuana is a green or gray mixture of dried, shredded flowers and leaves of the hemp plant *Cannabis sativa*. There are well over 200 slang or street terms for marijuana including "pot," "herb," "weed," "boom," "Mary Jane," "gangster," and "chronic." It is usually smoked as a cigarette (after being rolled in cigarette paper the old-fashioned way, called a "joint" or a "nail") or in a pipe or a bong. It is also used in "blunts" (cigars that have been emptied of tobacco and refilled with marijuana, often in combination with other drugs, such as crack cocaine). Some users mix it into foods or brew it as a form of tea.

The primary active chemical in marijuana is delta-9-tetrahydrocannabinol (T.H.C.). The membranes of certain nerve cells contain protein receptors that bind the T.H.C. This starts a series of cellular reactions that ultimately lead to the high that users experience when they smoke the drug.

The short-term effects of marijuana usage include problems with memory and learning, distorted perceptions, difficulty in thinking and problem-solving, loss of coordination, increased heart rate, anxiety and panic attacks.

Marijuana is usually smoked. The effects are felt within minutes and peak in ten to thirty minutes. They may linger for two to three hours. Low doses tend to induce a sense of well-being and a dreamy state of relaxation, which may be accompanied by a more vivid sense of sight, smell, taste and hearing, as well as the subtle alterations in thought formations and expressions. This state of intoxication may not be too noticeable to an observer (except for the user's pungent odor), but driving, occupational or household accidents often result from a distortion of the time-and-space relationship and impaired coordination.

Stronger doses intensify reactions. Users may experience shifting sensory imagery, rapidly fluctuating emotions, flights of fragmentary thoughts with distorted associations, an altered sense of self-identity, impaired memory and a dulling of attention (despite an illusion of heightened insight). Image distortion, loss of personal identity, fantasies, and hallucinations are also common side effects.

Marijuana contains known toxins and cancer–causing chemicals that are stored in fat cells for many months. Marijuana users also experience the same health problems as tobacco smokers, such as bronchitis, emphysema and bronchial asthma. Other effects include increased heart rate, dryness of the mouth, reddening of the eyes, impaired motor skills and concentration, frequent hunger and an increased desire for sweets and sugar. Extended use increases the risk to the lungs and reproductive system, as well as the suppression of the immune system. Hallucinations, fantasies and paranoia are also reported.

Long-term use by males results in the growth of breasts. Researchers have found that T.H.C. changes the way in which sensory information gets into and is acted on by the hippocampus. This is a component of the brain's limbic system that is crucial for learning, memory and the integration of sensory experiences with emotions and motivations. Investigations have shown that neurons in the information-processing system of the hippocampus and the activity of the nerve fibers are suppressed by T.H.C. In addition, learned behaviors also deteriorate.

Regarding the negative effects on user's lungs, a daily cough and phlegm as well as more frequent chest colds are common. Continued use of marijuana leads to abnormal functioning of lung tissues injured or destroyed by the smoke. Regardless of the T.H.C. content, the amount of tar inhaled by marijuana smokers and the level of carbon monoxide absorbed are approximately five times greater than among tobacco smokers.

In my work, I've heard just about every sorry excuse and explanation that the mind can dream up, and we often hear people saying that marijuana use is harmless and not addictive. My response is that a drug is addicting if it causes compulsive, often uncontrollable drug cravings, seeking, and use even in the face of negative health consequences. Marijuana meets this criterion. More than 150,000 people each year seek treatment for their primary marijuana addiction, and studies indicate that the drug causes physical dependence.

Anabolic Steroids

Anabolic steroids are synthetic substances related to the male sex hormones (androgens). They promote growth of skeletal muscle (anabolic effect) and the development of male sexual characteristics (androgenic effects) in females. Anabolic steroids are used by physicians to treat conditions that occur when the body produces abnormally low amounts of testosterone, such as delayed puberty and some types of impotence, and also used to treat "body wasting" in patients with AIDS or other diseases.

Legally available in the United States only by a prescription, anabolic steroid abusers obtain drugs that have been made in clandestine laboratories (often with poor quality control standards), smuggled in from other countries, or illegally diverted from U.S. pharmacies (stolen).

In the United States, supplements such as dehydroepiandrosterone (DHEA) and androstenedione (with the street name of "Andro") can be purchased legally without a prescription from many commercial sources, including health food stores. They are often taken because the user believes they have anabolic effects.

Anabolic steroid abuse is increasing among adolescents, and most rapidly among females. Increases of to 50 percent have been reported from the years 1992 to 2000, and now in 2012, the overall use has jumped another 22 percent.

Anabolic steroids are taken orally as tablets and capsules (Anadrol – oxymetholone, Oxandrin – oxandrolone, Dianabol – methandrostenolone, Winstrol – stanozolol, and others), by injections into muscles (DECA-Durabolin – nanodrolone decanoate, Durabolin – nandrolone phenpropionate, Depo-testosterone – testosterone cypionate, Equipoise – boldenone undeclyenate and others), or by ointment preparations rubbed into the skin. Doses taken by abusers can be up to 100 times more than doses for treating medical conditions.

In combination, a practice called "stacking," abusers take two or more anabolic steroids together, mixing oral and/or injectable types, and sometimes adding drugs such as stimulants or painkillers. The rationale for stacking is a belief that the different drugs interact to produce a greater effect on muscle size than could be obtained by simply increasing the dose of a single drug.

In cyclic dosage regimens, called "pyramiding," the abuser starts with a low dose of the stacked substance and gradually increases the doses for six to twelve weeks. In the second half of the cycle, the doses are slowly decreased to zero. And this is sometimes followed up by a cycle of conditioning training without using any drugs. Abusers believe that pyramiding gives the body time to adjust to the high doses, and the drug-free cycle allows time for the body's hormonal system to recuperate. As with stacking, the perceived benefits of pyramiding have not been substantiated.

Anabolic steroid user health consequences are far reaching. For boys and men, there is reduced sperm production, shrinking of testicles, impotence, difficulty or pain in urinating, baldness and irreversible breast enlargement (gynecomastia). For girls and women, there is the development of more masculine characteristics, such as decreased body fat and breast size, deepening of the voice, excessive growth of body hair and loss of scalp hair, as well as clitoral enlargement. In adolescents of both sexes, there is a premature termination of the adolescent growth spurt, so that the rest of their lives abusers remain shorter than they would have been without the drugs. In men and women of all ages, there are potentially fatal liver cysts and liver cancer, blood clotting, cholesterol changes and hypertension (each of which can produce heart attacks and strokes), and acne.

Anabolic steroid abuse can promote aggression that manifests itself as fighting, physical and sexual abuse, armed robbery and property crimes such as burglary and vandalism. Upon stopping anabolic steroid use, abusers can experience symptoms of depressed mood, fatigue, restlessness, loss of appetite, insomnia, reduced sex drive, headaches, muscle and joint pain and the increasing desire to take more anabolic steroids.

In addition to what these drugs alone can do, users risk infections resulting from the use of shared needles or nonsterile equipment, such as HIV/AIDS, hepatitis B and C, and infective endocarditis, a potentially fatal inflammation of the inner lining of the heart. Bacterial infections can develop at the injection site causing pain and abscesses.

Inhalants

According to Drug Enforcement Administration sources, inhalants are a chemically diverse group of psychoactive substances composed of organic solvents and volatile substances commonly found in nearly 2,000 everyday household products such as glue, hair spray, air fresheners, lighter fluid and assorted paint products. While not regulated under the Controlled Substances Act, many states have placed restrictions on the sale of these products to minors.

Inhalants can be sniffed directly from an open container or "huffed" from a rag soaked in the substance and held to the face. Alternatively, the open container or soaked rag can be placed in a bag where the vapors concentrate before being inhaled. The extensive capillary surface of the lungs allows rapid absorption of the inhaled substances, and inhalation causes blood levels peak rapidly. Entry into the brain is so fast that the effects of inhalants can resemble the intensity and effects produced by intravenous injection of other psychoactive drugs.

The effects of inhalant intoxication resemble those of alcohol inebriation, such as stimulation and loss of inhibitions, followed by depression. Users report distortions of perceptions of time and space, headaches, nausea and vomiting, slurred speech, loss of motor control and coordination and wheezing. A characteristic glue–sniffer's rash around the nose and mouth may be seen. An odor of paint solvents on clothes, skin and breath is often a sign of inhalation abuse.

Sniffing highly concentrated amounts of the chemicals in solvents and aerosol sprays can directly induce heart failure and death[62]. These chemicals can also cause death from suffocation by displacing oxygen in the lungs and then in the central nervous system, causing breathing to cease. I will always remember the thirteen-year-old boy I found sitting on a grassy hillside off of a dirt road in Virginia with a paper bag stuck to his face. He had been inhaling model airplane glue. The boy had bright red hair and a mass of freckles on his face. According to the medical examiner, he had been dead for about four hours before I found him.

The chronic use of inhalants has been associated with a number of serious long-term, and often irreversible health problems, including loss of hearing, brain and central nervous system damage, bone marrow damage, reduced sight and blindness in some cases, liver and kidney damage and blood depletion.

If you suspect that your child or friend, or other family member is using an inhalant—or any other drug—you must seek help right away. You cannot afford the luxury of waiting to see what may or may not happen. If you wait, someone could die.

Warning Signs

If there are friends or family members whom you suspect to be drug abusers, help is available to you. A good first choice is to call the local telephone number for the substance-abuse center nearest you. Whatever you do, don't ignore the warning signs. Get competent assistance right away.

Here are some of the signs that could indicate the use of drugs:

> ➤ Tracks or needle marks (usually on the arms, hands, legs or neck)

---

[62] PDR Staff. *Physician's Desk Reference*. Montvale, NJ: PDR Staff, 2011. Print.

➤ The wearing of long-sleeve shirts in warm weather (to hide needle marks)

➤ The wearing of sunglasses (to conceal dilated, constricted or bloodshot eyes)

➤ Long stays in the bathroom (possible drug ingestion)

➤ Frequent lateness to work or appointments (typical pattern of drug users)

➤ Excessive use of breath mints (masks the smell of alcohol)

➤ Unwarranted laughter (associated with marijuana or PCP use)

➤ Extreme mood swings (typical reaction to drug use)

➤ Unusually disheveled or unkempt appearance (distorted priorities)

➤ Nodding off (drowsiness or lethargy)

➤ Sweating profusely, even on cold days (physical reaction to drug use)

➤ Bad attitude in the morning (hangover, depression)

➤ Low self-esteem (often a sign of drug use)

➤ Borrowing or begging for money (to support a drug habit)

➤ Stealing (Items are pawned for cash to support a drug habit.)

➤ Poor circulation (reaction related to drug use)

➤ Undependable and/or unpredictable behavior (typical patterns of drug use)

- ➤ Aggressive, paranoid or "up-tight" behavior (common reaction to stimulants)

- ➤ Swollen or puffy hands and/or feet (signs of possible IV use)

- ➤ Constant sniffling (signs of withdrawal or nasal damage, also signs of cocaine being snorted)

- ➤ Yawning (withdrawal symptoms)

- ➤ Associating with known users (could indicate drug involvement)

- ➤ "Hanging out" in drug locations (could indicate drug involvement)

- ➤ Teary eyes (withdrawal symptoms)

- ➤ Unnecessary or obvious lying (to cover up drug use)

- ➤ Burns, lesions, sores in the mouth or on the lips (symptoms of smoking drugs)

- ➤ Burns or scorch marks on the nose, lips or face (the smoking of drugs)

- ➤ Burns on fingers, clothing, furniture and carpets (could indicate handling fire while high)

- ➤ Frequent isolation (low self-esteem; withdrawal from society; drug effects)

- ➤ Hyperactivity (possible stimulant use)

- ➤ Listlessness (withdrawal symptoms)

- ➤ Hiding liquor in unusual places (to conceal alcohol abuse)

- ➤ Presence of drug paraphernalia (signs of drug use/involvement)

- ➢ Smell of marijuana (use and/or association with users)

- ➢ Gradual disappearance of valuables (stealing)

- ➢ Unexplained spending of unusual amounts of money (could indicate drug involvement)

- ➢ Burnt spoons or bottle caps (items used to cook drugs)

- ➢ Knotted shoestrings or pantyhose (arm ties for IV use)

- ➢ Bloodstained water in the toilet or sink or bloody tissues (could indicate IV use)

- ➢ Drug-related illness (AIDS, endocarditis, abscesses, pneumonia, bronchitis, hepatitis, kidney failure, liver damage)

So, what's the solution? Simply, like it or not, you must stay involved with your children's activities, and if there is the slightest suspicion that they may be planning to attend a "rave" or "trance" you must stop them.

Offer alternatives; seek counseling; attend drug awareness seminars with your child. It doesn't matter what it takes — whatever it takes, just do it. You could be disliked intensely by your teenager for a while. That is understandable, but it doesn't matter. He'll get over it and in the long run will come to appreciate beyond words what you've done for him.

You must also get the police involved. If you suspect there will be a "rave" or "trance" taking place somewhere, call the police and let them know. They should make every effort to stop these types of gatherings, but they need your input. You must get involved.

Chapter Nineteen

Safety Tips for Field Employees

On a number of occasions, I have been asked to provide a safety list for the folks who have to go out into the neighborhoods and communities to conduct their business. As a result, I contacted the Security Management Bulletin of Waterford, Connecticut, and together we managed to provide a checklist of safety precautions that employees should think about before going out into the field[63]. You will find that much of this has already been touched upon, but the following list may help to reinforce those concepts:

Tips to Avoid an Assault:

➤ Project the image of a strong, confident person — someone who is awake and aware.

➤ Use your eyes; be aware of your surroundings. Avoid situations that seem dangerous. Trust your instincts.

➤ When faced with danger, stay as calm as possible. Think rationally and evaluate your options.

➤ If people attempt to alert you to possible danger, listen to them.

➤ Listen for unusual sounds, including footsteps behind you. If you're being followed while walking, cross the street and consider going in the opposite direction. Walk to a place where there are likely to be other people, or get back in your vehicle and leave the area right away.

➤ If your employer is sending you somewhere that seems dangerous, let your supervisor or manager know of your concerns. Again, always trust your instincts.

---

[63] Kephart, Stanley. *Security Management Bulletin*. Waterford, CT: Simon and Shuster, 1993. Print.

> In potentially dangerous situations, call the police. Ask for assistance from other employees so that you don't have to go somewhere alone.

> Do not carry cash or valuables. Flashing any amount of cash will grab the attention of a criminal.

> Be courteous and always show customers your company identification when you greet them. This will help to keep things on a friendly basis.

Tips for Vehicle Security:

> Check the vehicle before making calls. Make sure that the oil, water and tires are in proper order, and always keep the gasoline tank at least half full. All this will help to avoid breakdowns in undesirable areas.

> If you have an appointment in one of those undesirable areas, try to make it for relatively early in the morning. The idiots who would normally cause you problems will probably still be asleep or unconscious somewhere.

> Have your dispatcher verify all after-hour calls. A late call could very possibly be from someone trying to line you up for a robbery. Some taxi drivers know this all too well.

> While driving, watch for vehicles following you. They may be waiting for you to stop at a service call.

> Park as close to your destination as possible, but try to avoid alleys, parking lots and isolated side streets. Try to stay within eyesight of as many people as possible.

> Look around for suspicious people and situations before you leave your vehicle. Return to your appointment later if you feel uneasy for any reason. You can also call the police.

> When you leave your vehicle, lock the doors and roll the windows up.

> Use all of the vehicle's available lighting, such as headlights, rotating light and hazard lights. Regardless of what you may have heard or read elsewhere, I don't recommend using the interior lights during these types of situations.

> While returning to your vehicle, have the door key ready in your hand. You remember this drill, right? Look all around and under your vehicle as you approach it. Check the back seat, or rear cargo area before getting in. Do not approach your vehicle if someone unknown to you is in it or near it. Call the police right away.

> Finish all of your paperwork in a well-lit area away from the call, or back at the office.

What to do During an Assault:

> Stay calm and try to assure the assailant that you will follow all instructions. The assailant will most likely be very edgy, so try not to upset the idiot any more than is necessary.

> Tell the assailant exactly what you're going to do before making any moves. For example, "I'm getting out my wallet," or "I'm taking off my watch."

> If he asks for money, it might be better to give it to him. Do not offer rings, watches or jewelry, etc., unless he asks.

> Make a mental note of your assailant's appearance, including his height, approximate age, weight, eye and hair color, clothing and weapon description, as well as any possible vehicle he may be using and the direction of in which he leaves. Call the police immediately.

- ➢ If approached by an assailant, keep reassessing the situation and be aware if it begins to deteriorate. Possible responses, depending on the assailant's manner, include negotiating, stalling for time, distracting or diverting the assailant and then fleeing, screaming to attract attention and help from people nearby and physically resisting and fighting off the assailant.

- ➢ Please remember in the advice in Chapter One. It's important to understand that physical resistance should be a last resort tactic used when your life is in immediate danger.

What to do After an Assault:

- ➢ Call the police right away.

- ➢ Call your supervisor.

- ➢ Identify any witnesses. The police will want to interview them.

- ➢ Write down as soon as possible any possible description of the assailant, weapon, vehicle, and direction of travel, before you forget.

- ➢ Protect any evidence. Latent fingerprints can be obtained from any items touched by the assailant, such as your wallet and your vehicle.

- ➢ Carry an extra set of car keys so that if your assailant took your keys, you are not stranded.

- ➢ Do not make statements to the media. Tell any reporters who approach you to either check with the police or your company's public affairs office.

➢ Complete an incident report as soon as possible. This provides law enforcement agencies with important information. They might ask you to complete a written affidavit. Complete this right away.

Chapter Twenty

A Final Review

We've discussed a great many issues dealing with the effects of criminal activity and some of the simple steps we can take to safeguard our lives in various circumstances. Here is a review of some of the key points in this book, as well as some additional safety measures to help reinforce those concepts

General Advice

One of the best defensive tools against any kind of crime is your frame of mind. Work on building your self-confidence. Knowledge, awareness, good common sense and believing in yourself and your survival instincts will get you safely through most unpleasant circumstances.

We are much more likely to become the victims of theft than violence. And violence is much more likely to come from the hands of an acquaintance than those of a stranger. Adjust any fears you may have accordingly, and redirect those feelings of fear into good positive awareness.

Have a plan. Many criminals have spent hours formulating their plans in a loose sense and they sort of know ahead of time what they're going to do. They count on the fact that their victims will be unprepared and unable to react. The majority of them are cowards, and if they thought for a moment that you were prepared and able to react, they wouldn't try to victimize you in the first place. Learn all you can now (you've already taken a fantastic step in that direction by reading this book) and eliminate their ability to surprise you.

Share your newfound understanding of the issues in this book with your family and friends. Include your children in the discussions about avoiding crime. The more they know now, the better prepared they will be later on.

Remember that many, if not most, crimes are opportunistic in nature. Removing those opportunities will eliminate most criminal activity.

Compile a list of the things that concern you. If you have a fear about a specific type of criminal activity but don't know much about it, contact your local police department. They probably have at least one officer assigned to public relations duties, and he or she would likely be more than happy to meet with you about those concerns.

To help keep your neighborhood safe, schedule a meeting with your neighbors and friends, including your family, to really discuss the issues of burglary and other crimes. Together you can get fresh ideas about ways to keep your family and home safe. This type of brainstorming only helps; it's never a waste of time.

Make sure to involve your children in these discussions, sharing the issues in a matter-of-fact approach. If children are taught the issues of home and neighborhood safety in the same way they are taught fire safety or wearing seat belts in the car or wearing a helmet while riding a bicycle, they will accept the concepts quite readily.

Consider calling your local police department (at their nonemergency telephone number) to have them conduct a survey of your home security. They normally will have an officer respond to your needs whenever it's convenient for you. You can also use the checklist at the end of this chapter. Again, involve your children in this process. If you wish, they can walk along with the officer during the survey.

For a free catalog of additional safety information, you can write or call the National Crime Prevention Council, at:

> 1700 K Street NW
> Second Floor
> Washington, D.C. 20006-3817
> (800) WE-PREVENT)

For a booklet in Spanish, you can call (800) 727-UNETE.

Children can obtain a variety of comic and coloring books from:

> McGruff,
> Chicago, Illinois 60601

Protecting Property and Possessions

Most law enforcement agencies sponsor "Operation Identification" programs, where they offer kits for people to mark their valuable items. The kits normally contain electric engraving tools that can be used and then returned to the police department. Invisible ink markers are also available and can be used to mark things such as antiques or art work, or perhaps items of clothing, such as for coats.

Marking your valuables helps protect them because some thieves will not steal marked items, and pawn shops will not purchase anything with visible personal identification marks. (You may want to mark those items with your driver's license number and the two-letter state abbreviation, as opposed to using your Social Security number.) Also, if stolen property is recovered by the police it can be easily returned to the owners if it's marked, and if the thief is caught with the marked items, he can more easily be charged with the appropriate crime.

The "Operation Identification" program also provides small window stickers that can be used to advertise the fact that all of your valuable items have been marked. Place the stickers on the most obvious windows and doorways for potential burglars to see.

To help further protect your property, you should not only mark anything of value, but also take a periodic inventory of your property. Taking photographs of your property is an excellent idea. Photos can assist the police department in a theft and/or burglary case, and are also helpful to you and to the insurance company when you're trying to get reimbursed for the stolen property.

Valuable items such as televisions, DVD players and any other electronic components have serial numbers assigned to them. They are clearly readable on the manufacturer's plate (normally found on the bottom or the back of the item). During your inventory, make sure to include the serial numbers, as well as the model numbers and make of the item. All of this is extremely helpful to law enforcement and insurance companies. Police departments cannot enter your stolen DVD player (as an example) into the National Crime Information Center's (NCIC) computer banks without the serial number. So, if a thief is found in possession of the item, but the item is not in the computer, he may not be charged with the theft and you may never get the stolen item back.

If you own items that are extremely valuable, I recommend storing them in a safety deposit box at your bank. That's also a good place to store the inventory you took, as well as other important documents, such as copies of your passport and travel visa. (I have two of them, one here in the states and one overseas, with duplicate copies of documents.)

Keep Your Doings Private

Armed with more information than they need, criminals can easily take advantage of situations to find your home and possessions unattended.

First, there's no need to advertise where you live. As I've mentioned before, you should remove any sort of identifying tags from your key rings. Then, in the event that they are lost or stolen, you at least won't have the worry of somebody knowing where you live and what you drive.

If you're running a classified advertisement, make sure to use only your telephone number; do not list your address.

In the unfortunate circumstance of a death in your family, you might not want to list the dates and times that you will be attending church services, a viewing or the funeral itself. Believe it or not, criminals read the obituaries. And when they know that you will be off attending the funeral, they'll break into your home and steal anything they can. I recall the death of a very wealthy industrialist in Newport, Rhode Island, years ago. The funeral was a well-advertised event on the news and in the papers. Because of the family's collection of artwork and antiques at their estate, they thought there could be a problem, and called me for advice. I didn't have anyone to send to their estate at the time, so I ended up performing guard duties myself. If there is a death in your family, and it is in the newspapers, you may also want to have someone stay at your home while you're attending the services.

If you're planning a long-awaited vacation to the Caribbean, don't post it in the newspapers for everyone to read. (And don't post it on Facebook!) Some idiot will read that, look up your address and burglarize your home while you're away.

And as I've also mentioned, be very careful about what you talk about in public. Be cognizant of those around you. Talking in public with friends or family about the upcoming holidays to Bermuda could be overheard by others. And that bit of information can be used in unpleasant ways.

If you're trying to schedule a repairman or anyone to come to your house, do not go into any details about why Wednesdays (as an example) are not good for you. The repairman does not need to know that you're away every Wednesday.

After any sort of holiday or celebration, such as Christmas or someone's birthday, make sure that you dispose of all the boxes and gift wrapping. If they're placed at the curb in clear sight, it's an open invitation to thieves who realize that there's "new stuff" in that house. It's better to break the boxes down and get everything into large garbage bags.

Finally, I have heard the advice that everyone, including women, seniors and single people, should just use their first initial and last name on mailboxes or in the telephone book. That is bad advice. You should never have any part of your name on your mailbox or your house.

About Phones and Safety

If possible, you should have an unlisted telephone number, and here's the reason why: if your name appears on your mailbox, any criminal with half a brain can see the name, know the address, and then look you up in the telephone book and call your house. If you answer the telephone, you're obviously home. If you don't answer the telephone, the criminal might conclude that you're out shopping or at the office, and proceed to burglarize your house. Also, if they have your name and address, then get your telephone number out the phone book, they can call you up and try to scam you in some way. The less enlightened ones simply call to annoy you at all hours of the night and day. Having an unlisted telephone number is a good idea because it eliminates a great many of these problems.

If you receive obscene, harassing or annoying telephone calls, you should log the times the calls are made and then contact the police department right way to file a report. Also call the telephone company to either have your number changed to an unlisted number or to have a Caller Identification feature added to your system. It does cost a bit of money, but the benefits of seeing the name and telephone number of the person calling you before you answer the phone is well worth it. Having the combination of an unlisted number and the caller identification feature is the best approach.

If you can't afford to have an unlisted number or the caller ID system, at the very minimum, after having filed a police report, make sure that the telephone company changes your number. They will do that for you if you request it, and there are no charges to you because of the circumstances.

You can also screen calls with your answering machine, and only answer the calls when you know who's on the other line. By the way, if you do have a voice-mail system or an answering machine, never leave personal messages on it that give your name or say whether or not you're at home. You should leave a generic message, such as "You've reached 555-1212; please leave a message at the tone." If you're a single woman living alone, you may want to have a trusted male friend, your father or brother, record the message for you.

If you receive a wrong number call, do not volunteer any information to the caller such as, "No, this is the Smith's residence and the correct number is 555-1234." Simply say, "Sorry, but you have the wrong number," and let it go at that. Remember that criminals are looking for an advantage to either burglarize your home or victimize you in some other way.

You should make a list of emergency telephone numbers, such as the police, fire department, ambulance service and poison control, as well as your office, friends and neighbors. Post the list prominently at every telephone in your house. Make sure that your address and telephone number are displayed on that list. If you call 911 in an emergency, and the police or fire services in your area don't have the Enhanced 911 System installed, your address will not show on their computer screens. In an emergency you actually may not be able to remember your own address. To help first responders locate your house in the event of an emergency, post your house number (not your name) in well-lit clear areas on your house, your mailbox and perhaps even the curbing.

Never participate in telephone surveys. Most of those "surveys" are actually scams run by criminals. Do not give the callers any personal information. Simply say, "We're not interested — please never call this number again," and hang up. If the survey was legitimate (and that's sometimes doubtful), according to the law, whoever was calling you cannot call you back (and use "we're not interested" as opposed to "I'm not interested").

Never make purchases over the telephone if you're the one receiving the call. You may not know if the caller is legitimate or not. It's amazing how many people give away credit card information to strangers.

If you're away on vacation, leave your telephone in service. As I mentioned before, you may be able to monitor your incoming messages from a remote location and respond to the ones you feel are important. When I'm off on vacation, by the way, all I'm interested in is the sun and the sand. The telephone and the pager are left behind. I do carry a cell phone everywhere, however, just in case it's needed.

And speaking about cell phones — Did you know that all cell phone numbers are now public? This means that those numbers have been released to telemarketers, and you may well start to receive calls from those lovely people. You should know that you will be charged for each and every call you receive from telemarketers. To prevent that from happening, call the National Do Not Call list number from your cell phone, at 888-382-1222. The call you make to that number should only take a minute of your time, but it will be well worth it, as it blocks your number for five years. (You must make that call from your actual cell phone, not a different telephone.)

Here are four things you may not know about that cell phone of yours:

1. In times of grave emergencies, your cell phone can be a life saver or an emergency tool for survival. The worldwide emergency number for mobile phones, which includes the one you have, is 112. Memorize that number just like you did with 911. If you somehow find yourself out of your coverage area for your particular cell phone's mobile network, and it is a genuine emergency, dial 112. Your cell phone will search any existing network to establish the emergency number for you. This number can even be dialed if the keypad is locked. Dialing 112 will also link you directly to the state police or highway patrol for wherever you may be.

2. Your cell phone's battery contains hidden power. Yes, believe it or not, when your cell phone battery is low and perhaps not allowing you to make a call, in an emergency, simply press the following keys to activate that hidden power: 3370#. Your cell phone will then restart with this reserve power and it will show a 50 percent increase in battery power. That hidden reserve will get charged back up the next time you charge your cell phone.

3. You can disable a stolen mobile phone. If your cell phone gets stolen by one of the aforementioned lovely people roaming the planet, here's what you can do before it gets stolen: Check your mobile phone's serial number by keying in the following digits on your phone: *#06#. Remember, it must be precise: *#06#. A fifteen-digit code will appear on the screen. That fifteen-digit number is unique to your handset. Write the number down and keep it in a safe place. Then, if your cell phone gets stolen, you can call your service provider and give them that code. They will be able to instantly block that stolen phone from being used. Even if the thief changes the SIM card, the cell phone will be totally useless. You won't be getting your mobile phone back, but then again it's a small victory over the imbecile who stole it in the first place.

4. There is a free directory service for cell phones. Mobile phone companies are charging absurd amounts just for you dialing 411 for information. It is nothing more than thievery on their part, but there's a way around them. When you need to dial 411, dial 1-800-FREE411 instead (1-800-373-3411). The cell phone companies cannot charge you anything for this; it's a free service for you.

Protecting Your Credit Cards

The Basics

There are precautions we must all take if we are credit-card users. First, it's never a good idea to carry too many credit cards. Some people have up to eighteen or twenty cards and routinely carry them all. Carrying one or two is more than enough. Keep the rest of them in a safety deposit box.

Remember the inventory list you made with all those serial and model numbers? Make a list also with all your credit card information, including the numbers and expiration dates and keep that in your safety deposit box as well.

Remember to never write down your personal identification number (PIN) on or near the credit card, and don't use a PIN with obvious numbers, such as your birth date or Social Security number.

You may often receive offers for pre-approved credit cards in the mail. If you don't want the cards, make sure that those offers are torn up before you throw them in the trash. Most of those offers simply need a signature and, with a change of address noted on the return form, a credit card in your name can end up in the hands of someone else. You should know also that once you take your trash to the curb for pickup, it's fair game for anyone. If it's sitting on the curb, it's perfectly legal for anyone to come along and take your bag of trash.

If your credit card has expired, or if you're closing the account, make sure that you cut up the card. Concentrate on cutting up the parts that contain the card number and your name into very small pieces. Also, if your card is due to expire and you have yet to receive the new one, call the lending institution right away.

Carefully check your monthly credit card statements before sending out a payment. It's amazing just how many people will write a check for the amount due without having first read over the credit card purchases. If your credit card is missing or if there are any unfamiliar purchases on your statement, contact the issuing bank or company right way.

Use extreme caution when loaning your credit cards to anyone. I would loan my cards to my daughters, but that's about it. Make sure that you keep any receipts for purchases made with your credit cards.

Using Your Card

When making a store purchase with a credit card, make sure that the total amount on the slip is correct before signing it, and make sure also that the clerk hands you back your credit card and not someone else's. Switches of this kind are more common than you may realize.

Never allow a store clerk to use your credit card number as a guarantee on a check you wrote for a purchase or service. That is a violation of the law and the clerk should be reported to the police and the store manager.

Don't use your credit card for purchases conducted over the telephone if you didn't initiate the call.

No matter where you use your credit card, make sure that the person you're paying doesn't make any mistakes with the validation of your card. If you hear the words, "Oops," or "Let's try that again," be aware that you may be in the process of being victimized. What often happens here is that a clerk may try to run your card through the imprint device (to get the credit card numbers on the receipt for your signature) and tell you that, "It didn't take," or words to that affect, so that it has to be done again. If that happens, make sure you get the "bad" receipt; don't allow the clerk to keep it. Also, obtain all of the carbon copies. Someone may offer to tear them up and throw them away, but it's much better for you to retain everything you can. Remember that there are lots of places where all the computer technology that we take for granted is not in place or not being used, and they still use the imprint devices.

Here's a piece of advice about a specific credit card: You should know that the Discover card is worthless in most places abroad, so if you have one and you travel, you should just leave it at home.

Some Final Credit Card Tips

> Do not sign the back of your credit cards — ever. Instead, on the back in that signature bar write, "PHOTO ID REQUIRED." When making a purchase at a shop, the clerk can then just ask to see your driver's license, and that's perfectly legal. This way, if your card is ever stolen, the thief will not have your signature. If he gets your signature, he could very easily forge your signature on other documents.

> When you write checks to pay off or pay down your credit card bill, never, ever, put the complete account number on the memo line. Instead of that, write down the last four digits of the credit card number. Your credit card company knows the rest of the numbers, and no one (including banking personnel) who might be handling your checks as it goes through all the processing channels will have access to them.

➤ Put your work telephone number on your checks instead of your home number. If you have a post office box, use that address instead of your street address on your checks. If you don't have a post office box, consider using your work address. Never, ever, put your Social Security number on your checks.

➤ Photocopy the contents of your wallet. Copy both sides of those credit cards, driver's licenses, etc. Keep the copies in a safe place, such as that safety deposit box at your bank I mentioned before. If your wallet is ever lost or stolen, you will have instant access to all those numbers, as well as the telephone numbers to call in order to cancel the cards.

➤ If your credit card is stolen, file a police report immediately in the jurisdiction where you believe it was taken. In other words, if it was stolen while you were in Atlanta, Georgia, don't wait until you get back to Boston, Massachusetts, and try to file a report with the Boston Police Department. They'll tell you to contact the Atlanta Police. Filing a report immediately proves to credit providers that you were diligent, and that is the first step in any possible investigation.

➤ If your credit card is stolen, call the three national credit reporting agencies right away to place a fraud alert on your name; also call the Social Security fraud line number. Don't wait one minute to do this, it is so very important. If a thief has your credit cards, he more than likely will use them as soon as he can. He knows that they'll be cancelled soon, so he's going to spend like a drunken Russian sailor in those first few hours.

Here are the numbers you'll need:

Equifax, 1-800-525-6285

Experian, 1-888-397-3742

Trans Union, 1-800-680-7289

Social Security Administration fraud line,1-800-269-0271

Frauds and Scams

There are an abundance of people in this world eager to part you from your money. The following are a few of the more common scams and swindles:

> Bargain price repairs on seeming costly home improvements.

> Work-at-home schemes requiring an up-front investment from you.

> Eyeglass or hearing aid offers

> Long-term insurance or health insurance schemes

> Debt reconsolidation schemes or claims against debts you don't remember incurring.

> Remedies and cures for various illnesses or ailments

> Any investment scheme with a high expected return (absolutely impossible to guarantee).

The word to the wise: if an offer seems too good to be true, it probably is. And as I advised earlier — and it can't be emphasized enough — be extremely wary of people trying to approach you on the street. Don't believe anything they tell you. The bottom line is that they want your money. Report any suspicious activity or people to the police right away.

As I've mentioned before, financial transactions offer a prime opportunity for people to scam you. Here a couple of ideas to help you avoid the more common scenarios:

> Have your regular paychecks, pension or retirement checks as well as your Social Security checks deposited electronically into your bank account. This will guarantee that they are deposited in a timely manner and will avoid the possibility of lost or stolen checks. This also saves you from those extra trips to the bank, where you could be exposed to someone trying to take advantage of you.

> If you make a withdrawal from your bank account for any large amount of money, consider getting it in the form of a money order or a cashier's check. Carrying either one is much safer than carrying cash, and they are perfectly negotiable. If you're traveling, consider carrying traveler's checks. These can be cashed anywhere, and if lost or stolen will be replaced right away by the financial institution that issued them.

Protecting Children

Unfortunately, we live in a world where evil things happen. I truly believe that our children are gifts from God, but I also know that there are evil people in this world, pedophiles and the like, who want nothing more than to have an opportunity with a child. In my opinion, these people are horrible monsters who must be removed from society; they cannot be rehabilitated. God, I'm sure, has a special hell for them, but we have to deal with the realities of the here and now.

You must not allow these people to have access to your children. Pedophiles attempt to lure children, using techniques like asking a child for help (trying to find a lost puppy, or getting directions) or telling a child that there's an emergency (their mother's been taken to the hospital, or their house is on fire), all in an attempt to get at the child, or have the child get close enough to their car so that they can be taken. Children must be made aware of these things. It won't do any good to really frighten your child with all the awful details, but they must be aware of the dangers.

The best thing you can do to protect your children is to be there for them. Be a responsible parent. Know to the minute what your child's schedule is. Instill in your children the understanding that they must call you right away if there are any changes to the normal schedule. There can be no exceptions to this rule.

Know what time your child is expected to be on and off the school bus, and the time it takes them to get to the front door. Make meeting your child at the bus stop a priority, but if you're unable to meet the school bus for some reason, at least monitor the time. If they're even only a couple of minutes late, be concerned. If they're more than ten minutes late, you'd better call the police immediately.

Make it crystal clear to the school or activity leader, or whoever has the responsibility to care for your child, that you are to be called immediately if your child does not arrive at school, or is missing.

If the worst happens and your child is abducted, you must act immediately. Police have a much better chance of safely recovering your child within those first few minutes to an hour or so. Any amount of time beyond that, and getting your child back safely will be a miracle.

Know the routes your children take when they walk anywhere, whether to school or to a friend's house. Walk those routes with them and note any areas of concerns or trouble spots. Children always seem to find out where the short-cuts are, but make sure that they don't stray from those safe routes (if they are indeed safe).

Consider purchasing bracelet-style GPS devices that your children can wear. These things are absolutely fantastic. If you're concerned about the whereabouts of your child, you simply hit a button on your GPS receiver, and it will tell you instantly where your child is (as long as he or she is wearing the device). It gives you the coordinates of your child, and a police officer can immediately respond to that location.

You might want to get your neighbors involved in keeping neighborhood children safe. You could organize a neighborhood meeting to decide if there is a location, such as one of the neighbors' homes, for a safe house. In this context, a safe house is a place where a child can go if he feels threatened in some manner. This would be especially useful on occasions when you may not be home for some reason, and your child is playing somewhere in the neighborhood and needs a place to go to right away. Make sure that the safe house is in the home of people you know and trust. If a single male offers his house as a safe house, decline the offer. (Better to have your child avoid that location entirely.)

Teach your child what to do if he is threatened. Earlier in this book I mentioned the benefits of screaming. Screaming is an important tool, and one that can save your child from harm. Every parent can attest to the fact that children are terrific screamers. (As a matter of fact, they could probably teach us a thing or two about it!) Let your children know that not only is it alright to scream under certain circumstances, but that they're really *supposed* to scream when confronted with danger. Conduct a practice session; make it a family or neighborhood project. (If you're conducting practice sessions in your home, let the neighbors know so they won't be alarmed. And if you're conducting a neighborhood scream-off, make sure that the police are informed beforehand. The last thing you need is two or three patrol cars skidding to a halt right in front of you!)

For more information about protecting your children, write to:
Child Lures
2119 Shelburne Road,
Shelburne, Vermont 05842

You can also contact:
The National Center for Missing and Exploited Children
2101 Wilson Boulevard, Suite 550
Arlington, Virginia 22201

Safeguarding Your Home

This book has gone into great detail about the things you can do to help safeguard your house from burglaries. I've talked about lighting, but let me just add that the more lighting you install around the exterior of your home, the better. Remember that lights should be the motion-sensor type and should be placed about nine feet off of the ground. Adding other types of lights is helpful as well. Walkway lights, patio lights, floodlights and spotlights all help to dissuade potential burglars.

Here are some other strategies to consider:

➢ Gravel walkways are terrific. Where I grew up in England, nearly everyone had them. I think they're rather good to look at, and they also offer some measure of safety. I've had more than one burglar tell me that they avoid homes surrounded by gravel or pebble walkways because of the noise the gravel makes when anyone is walking or driving over it.

➤ You can hang small bells, like reindeer or sleigh bells, from gates and doorways as well as windows. They are quite decorative and offer another simple and inexpensive safety feature to your home. Anything that makes extra noise, metal as opposed to plastic, is good.

➤ I've talked about the importance of alarm systems and having alarm system signs displayed. You can also purchase from most hardware stores stick-on strips of tape that have small wires running through them, for the mere price of about $5. Attach these to the inside of your windows where they can be seen from the outside. It'll look just like an alarm system wiring job, and the idiot burglar won't have any way of knowing it's not the real thing.

➤ During the Christmas season, we all have our Christmas trees up and lit. But remember, this is also the time when burglars are especially active. If you have a sizable bunch of presents under your tree and they're clearly visible from the outside, burglars will be tempted. We love to show off our lighted trees to the neighborhood, but just be careful about this. You may want to have those drapes drawn shut to conceal what's under the tree, or else bring the gifts out to put under the tree on Christmas Eve. At least in that way they are only there for one night.

➤ Another thing to consider are the small wall safes that come disguised as plug sockets or wall-mounted switch plates. They look just like the real thing, are inexpensive and relatively easy to install. They're great places to keep your jewelry and other small valuables hidden. They're not a bad little investment.

➤ Many thieves are trading in their old-fashioned lock picks for electronic devises called a "code grabbers." As you operate your garage-door opener with your remote control, the code grabber can capture the signal. And this can be done from several hundred feet away; you'll never know it happened. When you drive away, the burglar can transmit that captured signal to open your garage door. He then drives right in, closes the garage door behind him and helps himself to your possessions in relative seclusion. Thankfully, during the last few years, manufacturers have added effective code-blocking devices to garage-door openers. If your garage-door opener was manufactured before 1982, and a great many of them were, it should be replaced. Contact the manufacturer and find out about their replacement policy. Some of them will upgrade your system at no cost to you. And just remember that the garage door remote control is really a key to get in and out of your home. Treat it the same way you would the other keys — keep it safe and out of sight.

➤ One thing I haven't mentioned before is pet doors. You know, those small doors people install on one of their home's exterior doors. Believe it or not, some burglars actually use their children, or someone's child, to squeeze through pet doors and then unlock the regular door to let the burglar in. This happens quite often. Those pet doors really should not be more than six inches across. Any animal larger than that should be let in and out by the homeowner.

Home Security Checklist

Here is a checklist that you can use to help in securing your home:

➤ Are all the outside doors of the house of metal or solid wood construction?

➤ Are all the entrances to the living quarters from the garage and basement of metal or solid wood construction?

➤ Are all the door frames strong enough and tight enough to prevent forcing or spreading?

➤ Are the door hinges protected from removal on the outside?

➢ Are there windows in any doors or within 40 inches of a door?

➢ Are all the door locks adequate and in good repair? There's a product on the market called the Ultimate Lock, and it's available through your hardware store. It's designed to withstand more than 4,000 pounds of pressure; it can't be picked or pried; and it'll stop most burglars in their tracks. They're expensive, about $180 or so, but well worth the investment.

➢ Does the door from the garage to the living quarters have locks adequate for an exterior entrance?

➢ Is the garage door kept closed and locked at all times?

➢ Are the garage windows adequately secured for ground floor windows?

➢ Is the outside utility entrance to the garage as secured as required for ground floor entrances?

➢ Are all of the garage doors lighted on the outside?

➢ Does the door from the basement to the living quarters have adequate locks?

➢ Are strikes and strike plates adequate and properly installed?

➢ Can the door's locking mechanism be reached through a mail slot or pet entrance?

➢ Is there a screen or storm door with an adequate lock?

➢ Do all the windows have adequate locks in operating condition?

➢ Do the windows have screens or storm windows that lock from the inside?

- ➤ Do any windows open onto areas that may be hazardous or offer special risk of burglary?

- ➤ Do windows that open to hazardous areas have security screens or grills?

- ➤ Are the exterior areas to the windows free from concealing structure or landscaping?

- ➤ Are all the entrances lighted with at least 40-watt lights?

- ➤ Can the front entrance be observed from the street or public area?

- ➤ Does the porch or landscaping offer concealment or view from the street?

- ➤ Is there a sliding glass door? Is it secure against being lifted out of its track? Are there "Charley Bars" or other locking mechanisms being used on the sliders?

- ➤ Are trees and shrubberies trimmed back from the upper floor windows?

- ➤ Are tools and ladders secured somewhere out of the reach of burglars?

- ➤ Is there an exterior door leading to the basement? If so, is that door adequately secured for an exterior door? Is it adequately lighted?

- ➤ Is the outside basement door concealed from the street or the neighbors?

- ➤ Are all of the basement windows adequately secured against entry?

- ➤ Does the garage door have adequate locking devices?

> Are your house numbers clearly displayed and easily read from the street?

If you answered NO to any of those questions, you now know what to do to correct the problem.

Safeguarding Your Car and Its Contents

You may have heard the bad advice being given by some well-meaning people about how to park your car in the driveway. They say to park with the back in and the engine facing towards the street. The rationale is that it may be easier to see a thief trying to hot-wire your car when it's parked in this manner. But people fail to realize that many cars are stolen by simply being towed away. Parking your car with the engine facing towards the street actually helps a thief tow your car. It's a much better idea to park facing in, as most of us do, and then turn the steering wheel hard either to the left or the right before turning off the ignition.

Here are some other things to think about when it comes to safeguarding your car and the things that are in it:

> If you're selling your car privately don't allow anyone to take it for a test drive unaccompanied. You may never see the car again.

> Remember: keep things out of sight in your car—especially electronics or other high-value items. Thieves have been known to jump out from a hiding place while a car is at a stop sign or traffic light, bash in the car window, grab whatever is available and be off with it before the driver knows what happened. One way to do keep things hidden is to carry a small blanket or towel in the car, the same color as the carpeting, to cover any items such as groceries or department store purchases. It'll help make those items just a little less noticeable.

> If you have letters and bills lying on the front seat, try to put them in the glove box, out of sight. The information on them (your name and address) might be useful to a thief.

Personal Safety

As I've mentioned before, if you're home alone late at night and someone comes to your door, ignoring that knock on the door or the doorbell is not a good idea. It's an open invitation for a thief to try and break in. It's much better to call the police, then make as much noise as possible and turn on as many lights as you can. You don't have to open that door. Tell whoever is at the door that you're just "putting the dog away!" Make sure the police are en route.

You may have heard that if you're asleep and you're awakened by the sounds of someone either in your house or trying to get in, you should just stay in bed and pretend to be asleep. That's the *last* thing you want to do. Instead, you should immediately dial 911 and get the police there, fast. Lock your door and arm yourself. Make as much noise as you can while doing this; noise may scare off the intruder. Remember my earlier advice about keeping your car keys next to your bed? Push that car alarm button immediately. And the wasp and hornet spray we talked about—now's the time to grab for it.

When you're out and about, keep these things in mind to stay safe:

➢ Schedule your arrival time at bus and train stops to minimize your waiting time.

➢ Before you get into a bus or a taxi, or even the train, look inside. If you feel uncomfortable about what you see, trust your instincts and don't get in.

➢ Sit as close to the bus driver or conductor as possible. Keep your handbag, briefcase or any other items close to you and secure.

➢ Try not to use the public restrooms in malls and other similar places, and absolutely never allow your child to go into these facilities. Try to have those bathroom breaks taken care of ahead of time, or consider using a bathroom in a restaurant.

➤ If you're going shopping at a mall, try purchasing the least expensive items first, and leave the high-value items for the very last part of your shopping trip. Avoid being loaded down with lots of boxes and packages. Try to shop with a companion.

➤ Don't ever pick up hitchhikers, and don't be a hitchhiker.

Highway Safety

Keeping yourself safe while traveling on the highway deserves its own separate section. We've covered these points before, but they can't be emphasized enough. When it comes to highway safety, here are some important things to remember:

➤ Be sure to carry a cell phone when you're driving. It is probably the one most useful piece of emergency equipment you can have. Most violent crimes related to driving a car can be circumvented by the appropriate use of a cell phone. Program emergency numbers into it and keep it close at hand. Also, keep it charged up and turned on.

➤ Keep things in your car that could help in an emergency, including a blanket, some drinking water, a flashlight, a first aid kit, flares and jumper cables.

➤ Do not stop on off-ramps or in business lots at night and bury your head in a map (even if the area is well lit).

➤ Do not take off-ramps that bear the heavy graffiti tip-off that the area is either gang-controlled, or is an area where gangs are having an influence. Do drive on. Look for a police station, fire department or an open business in a safe area with no loiterers or graffiti.

➤ Remember that even if you're lost you are much safer in a moving car than when stopped.

➢ Have your passenger read the map while you continue to drive. If you need to change a tire, have the passenger diligently watch the area. Be ready to react to crime.

➢ If you're being followed, look in your rearview mirror. If you're suspicious that someone may be following you, do not go home or anywhere else you frequent (such as your office, school or gymnasium, to name a few). Instead, go to the police or fire department or to an open public place where it's well lit and there are lots of people. If someone does follow you there, try to record the license plate and also get a good description of the car and its occupants. As soon as it's safe, call the police.

➢ If you have a cell phone and you think that you're being followed, call the police and keep driving. Give them your locations as you go along, and describe your car. They will soon be there to assist.

➢ Avoid rest areas at night, especially if you're a female. These areas are havens for opportunistic criminals.

➢ If your car is bumped while you're driving, resist the urge to stop the car to view the damage. We're conditioned to do this, but don't. These ruses are often preludes to carjackings. They usually take place in parking lots, at stop signs or red lights, or even when you're driving along. They frequently take place at night when no one else is around, often in an urban area or any area that is sparsely traveled because of the late hour. As I've advised before, drive to an open business and call the police. You will not be charged with leaving the scene of an accident, because you left the area to call the police from a safe location. Here's an exception, though: if you look in that rearview mirror, and the driver who just bumped you is an elderly lady, it would then be appropriate to stop. Just use good common sense and be very careful, no matter what the situation may be.

➢ No matter what, never accept a ride from someone else. Remember, do not allow strangers to have access to you or to control you in any way.

➢ If your car breaks down and you are with other people, stay together. Never split your group up. Never leave someone behind or with the car. If you decide to walk to get help, go in a group. The only reason to leave your car is if you can actually see a destination where help may be available, such as an open business or a freeway telephone call-box (if you don't have a cell phone). If you do this, use caution. In the daytime, stay in your car with the doors locked and the windows rolled up.

➢ If your car breaks down on a sparsely traveled highway or roadway late at night, the best thing to do could actually be to leave your car, after you've called the police (on that cell phone!). Walking away from the roadway and into the woods at night may seem somewhat extreme, but even with the doors locked and the windows rolled up (in this scenario on that sparsely traveled road), criminals could get inside. If you're standing still or sitting in the woods, even just a few feet in the wood line, it would take a miracle for anyone to actually see you. If a car full of idiots were to stop and break into your car, let them. They're not going to see you in the woods being very still and quiet and they will eventually leave. If you sit still, you're as good as invisible. If a police officer comes along, then you can step out from your hiding place.

In case you're wondering if all these precautions are really necessary, let me share with you examples of three types of scams being used to take advantage of motorists. Warnings about these scams have been coming in from law enforcement agencies around the country.

1. A woman was driving down a rural road outside of Canton, Ohio, when she spotted an infant car seat on the side of the road. It had a blanket draped over it. Fortunately she didn't stop, but instead called the Canton Police Department. They sent officers to the location to check things out, but also informed her that gangs and thieves were plotting different ways to get cars to pull to a stop, hopefully with a woman behind the wheel. The morons will place infant car seats on the roads, sometimes with a lifelike baby doll inside, and wait for a woman to pull over. This usually occurs in a rural area, sometimes near woods or vacant fields, and the person who stops, usually a woman, will be dragged into the woods by the gang, beaten and raped, and very often murdered. Men, too, will be beaten and robbed and left for dead. Whatever you do, never stop if you see something like this. Instead, immediately call 911 on your cell phone and keep on driving. Do not even slow down.

2. If you're driving at night, you may have eggs thrown at your windshield. Do not stop to check your car. Do not operate your windshield wipers, and do not spray any water or windshield wiper fluid on them. Eggs mixed with water or windshield wiper fluid become milky and blocks your vision up to around 95 percent. If you stop, you will be victimized by these violent criminals. Call 911 right away on your cell phone, but keep driving, don't even slow down. And don't use your windshield wipers.

3. I've mentioned this one before, but it bears repeating. Sometimes criminals use cars with flashing lights and, posing as police officers, try to get motorists to pull over. If, while driving, you find yourself being "pulled over" by what you believe is an unmarked police car, do not stop. Using your cell phone, dial either 911, or 112 if you're out of your service area. Get the real police to you in a hurry. Just do NOT stop for that guy behind you.

Avoiding Road Rage

Driver etiquette is one of the best tools for avoiding incidents of road rage. Here are some things to remember:

> ➤ Let tail-gaiters pass. If someone insists in tailgating you, pull over to the outside (slow) lane, if it's possible, and let them pass. If you're driving on a four-lane roadway and the speed limit is 45 miles per hour, as an example, do not stay in the passing lane doing 45 miles per hour. Move over. Someone will most certainly come up behind you and that person is trying to drive 65 or 70 miles per hour. If you don't move over right away, or at the very least speed up and then move over as soon as possible, you could enrage the guy behind you.

> ➤ Most disputes between drivers can be avoided if you leave your "I'll fight for this piece of highway" attitude at home. Some males suffer from that affliction for some reason, but most instances of road rage can be avoided by using some common sense. If they want to go over the speed limit, let them. Allow them room to pass. You're not the state police and you don't need to monitor or enforce the speed laws either directly or with a rolling road block. We already have very good folks taking care of those matters.

> ➤ If you want to pull out onto a roadway from a side street or driveway, make sure that you don't pull out directly in front of someone and then drive so slowly that the other car is now right behind you. This is hazardous and you will be asking for trouble. It's much better to let them pass first and then pull out onto the roadway.

We live in the information age, and there is free information on crime prevention available from the National Crime Prevention Council located at:

1700 K Street, NW
Second Floor
Washington D.C. 20006-3817
or call them at (800) WE PREVENT

You can obtain their catalog and information booklets which can give you some additional insights into personal, home and business safety.

Chapter Twenty One

Conclusion

In his book, *In Pursuit of Happiness and Good Government,* Charles Murray wrote, "For lawfulness to exist, it is not necessary for the police to catch every lawbreaker. Nor need the punishment be severe. The only thing that is necessary is that when someone who commits a crime is arrested for it, his neighbors' perception of the world leads them to say, 'he is in big trouble.' If they say, 'he'll probably walk,' lawfulness doesn't exist.[64]" In many areas of America today, and in many parts of the world, lawfulness does not exist at all. On the contrary, lawlessness has taken root and has enveloped our lives.

Unlike Mr. Murray, I believe that punishments should reflect the severity of the crimes. I believe in the death penalty for certain crimes, and life in prison without the possibility of parole for certain other crimes. I do not believe in any form of early release for good behavior, time served or plea bargaining. I do believe that a twenty-year sentence as an example, should be twenty years and not one day sooner. And I don't think it does any good to have a convicted murderer sitting for years on death row while going through endless appeals. Give the murderer the opportunity for some appeals, and if the conviction is not overturned, complete the sentence.

Now, I'm reasonably sure that a few liberals reading this will be furious. "Oh my, just the thought that those poor misunderstood criminals will have to languish in prison for their full sentences positively makes my head swim." Look, you take anyone, including liberals, and have them become the victims of crime, and all of a sudden their views about criminals and their punishments change dramatically. I've seen this so many times. Some of them make such a dramatic 180-degree turn on these issues, it's truly amazing.

But my views and opinions aside, it is what you understand about all of this that's important. In the final analysis, we all have differing opinions, but regarding those issues that can adversely affect our lives we should, hopefully, be in unison.

---

[64] Murray, Charles. In *Pursuit of Happiness and Good Management*. New York: Simon and Shuster, 1994. Print.

I'll go back to what I wrote in the beginning: you must trust your instincts and listen to your fears. It will be your intuitions (your instincts) that will signal you when something is wrong, that danger is imminent. You can always rely on your intuition in two very important ways. First, your intuition will always appear in response to something. And second, your intuition always has your best interest at heart.

Now, before you think old Elliott has finally gone off the deep end, let me explain. Some years ago I investigated a rape case where the victim told me that there was absolutely nothing in the man's demeanor to explain the instinctive fear she felt when he first approached her. The man just didn't match her preconceived image of a rapist. Before the rape, the man was actually charming to her. (Remember, they don't all look like the murderers Charles Manson and Osama bin Laden.)

The victim said that the man insisted on helping her carry some packages from her car to her apartment door. He would not take "No" for an answer. She initially resisted, but he made her feel guilty. He was very talkative, used the word "we" more than once in order to create trust and an unconscious bond, and promised that he would just carry the bags to the door and then leave. She finally gave in to his insistence, and ended up being brutally raped.

Here are some things to remember about liars and criminals: People who lie to you, who want to deceive you in some way, will often use a technique I once heard referred to as the "Overwhelming Details" approach, or "O.D.," for short. A complete stranger may come up to you and begin a conversation. Be wary. Often during the course of this one-sided conversation he will inject a great deal of nonsensical detail. He does this because to him what is being said is not credible, and so he keeps talking. He's trying to overwhelm you with detail and distract you from what should be obvious.

To overcome this, you must remain conscious of the context in which details are offered. Criminals are liars, every last one of them. And if you instinctively know that someone is lying to you, you should also know that some sort of criminal intent may be at hand.

In the case of the rape victim, the rapist made her feel guilty when she initially refused his assistance. He did this in the way he spoke to her, and in the slightly critical way he spoke, "You're not one of those women's libbers are you?" Feeling a little guilty, she then accepted his offer of help. A man who intends to harm you will often label you in a slightly critical manner. This can be referred to as typecasting.

A good defense for this is to act as if the words were never spoken. You must be firm and deliberate. Use words like, "I said I do not need your help, now get away from me!"

The rapist initially used charm. Many criminals use this approach. You should think of charm not as a trait, but more like a verb. Tell yourself that, "This person is trying to charm me," as opposed to "This person is charming." You should then see through the deception.

The man made an unsolicited promise. He promised to leave as soon as he carried her packages to the apartment door. Those unsolicited promises are very real danger signals. Criminals use them because they know that victims may not be completely convinced of their sincerity.

When you say "No" to someone, and he ignores you, that person is trying to control you. He is also refusing to relinquish control. You must NEVER relent on the word "No." This is especially true with strangers. Never give ever-weakening refusals and then give in. Never let him think that you're open to negotiation. Be firm. You can say, "I said no, I don't want your help!"

Always remember, God has equipped us with all sorts of inner feelings and intuition. Listen to them. If you feel fear, know that it is a signal in the presence of danger. It is based on your perceptions of the environment. Always listen to true fear. It's our survival instinct and it works.

Now, just one last thought about that rape case. The criminal's approach to the victim with his unyielding offer of help had the effect of placing the victim in his debt. This technique tends to exploit the victim's sense of obligation, and it gives the criminal another opening. You must be aware of the two critical factors here. First, the man approached her. And second, she did not ask for his help.

This example was an absolutely brutal rape case. But the techniques used by this particular criminal are used in many crimes besides rape, including assault and battery, robbery, theft, fraud and many others.

I wish someone would open up a one-week camp or retreat devoted to training people about how to avoid becoming a victim of crime. It's unfortunate, but nevertheless a fact of life, that we live in a world where thousands of criminals roam free. If we all knew how to recognize them, how to avoid them and how to deal with them when they try to victimize us, we would be so much better off.

I would like to mention this just one more time before you close the covers to this book: Normally, as I stated in Chapter Ten, I don't usually recommend one particular Internet website above any others, because there are a great many sites on the Web designed to assist in various ways. But Family Watch Dog stands head and shoulders above the others, in my opinion. It can be accessed at: www.familywatchdog.us.

If you go to this site, you can type in your address and instantly find out if there are any registered sex offenders living near you. You simply point and click. If you find that a sex offender is living close by, you can instantly find his or her photograph, address, and usually the convictions with which he or she was charged. It's a free service and definitely well worth the small effort.

It was not my intent to frighten anyone with this book. Nor do I wish our society to become one where paranoia has taken root. My intent is to inform, to make us more aware, much more cautious, and to bring into focus some of the awful realities in our society. My sincere hope is that having read through these pages, you come away a much more confident and capable person.

www.ingramcontent.com/pod-product-compliance
Lightning Source LLC
Chambersburg PA
CBHW071337290326
41933CB00039B/1082

9780615766034